Merry Christmas
To: The Parkers
Love From: The Morrisons
1982.

THE GRAND HOMES OF TEXAS

THE GRAND HOMES OF TEXAS

FROM THE EDITORS OF TEXAS HOMES

EDITED BY ANN RICHARDSON/PHOTOGRAPHY BY HICKEY-ROBERTSON

Texas Monthly Press

Texas Monthly Press, Inc.
P.O. Box 1569
Austin, Texas 78767

A B C D E F G H

Library of Congress Cataloging in Publication Data

Richardson, Ann.
The grand homes of Texas.
1. Interior decoration—Texas—History—20th century. 2. Dwellings—Texas. I. Title.
NK2004.R52 747'.8883'09764 82-5748
ISBN 0-932012-36-1 AACR2

CONTENTS

ACKNOWLEDGMENTS

Texas Homes wishes to thank the following staff members for their contributions to our first book, *The Grand Homes of Texas.*

Judy Anderton, *Promotion Manager*
Juanita Barnes, *Art Director*
Lauri Beth Clark, *Art Production*
Betsie Bolger Day, *Associate Editor*
Betty Dillard, *Associate Editor*
Mariana C. Greene, *Editor*
Charles M. Ray, *Production Manager*
Deone Roe, *Production Assistant*
Lisa Ruffin, *Senior Editor*
Paula Skinner, *Typographer*
Suzanne Stavinoha, *Assistant Editor*

WRITERS

Betsie Bolger Day 125-133
Betty Dillard 173-183
Derro Evans 33-39
Anita Creamer Lund 143-153
Lisa Ruffin 3-13, 15-25, 41-49, 51-59, 79-89, 111-123, 135-141, 185-191, 201-207, 209-215, 217-225
Sandy Sheehy 27-31, 61-69, 71-77, 91-101, 103-109, 155-163, 165-171, 193-199

DESIGNED BY BARBARA LEE CHAPMAN

INTRODUCTION

On a crisp and almost blindingly bright spring day, I took the leisurely drive from Houston to a place called Chappell Hill—with good reason. My companion was my mother, and she had quite a story to tell. She told the story the way I'm sure her great-grandfather would have told it. About how he'd settled there in 1842; about the dust and the sun and the need to belong. That's how I came to understand the word home.

It's the need to belong. My great-great-grandfather found a way to belong amongst the pine needles and cottonmouths; over the ensuing decades, Texans have not fought the same foes, but they've fought with the same spirit. Whether carving out a bit of country-in-the-city in San Antonio, deciding how to make more out of less in a Dallas high rise or bringing a forgotten landmark back to life on the King Ranch, Texans understand a home is not just a house. As one homeowner said of homes in West Texas, "They are used for everything—our hotels, our restaurants, our tea rooms, our country clubs. They are where our children are born and where they marry."

As you tour *The Grand Homes of Texas*, I hope you will experience as I have the special quality of Texas homes and the Texans who have created them. My sincere thanks goes to these Texans for being so generous in sharing their beautiful homes with the editors of *Texas Homes*.

Ann Richardson
Publisher and Editor-in-Chief
Texas Homes

THE TEXAS GOVERNOR'S MANSION

It comes as a pleasant surprise, for so young and feisty a state, that the Texas Governor's Mansion is the fourth oldest in the country. Completed in 1856 after the legislature earmarked $17,000 to erect and furnish a permanent home in Austin for the state's governors, it stands as one of Texas' most significant buildings. Excepting an addition during the Colquitt Administration in 1914, there have been no structural alterations and only patchwork interior upgrading. "It's that uncertainty about running for a second term," laughs Mrs. William P. Clements, Jr. "Somehow, moving out of the Mansion for renovations the whole time you're in office isn't too attractive."

In 1982, for the first time since that addition, the Mansion threw open its noble doors revealing a much-changed monument to Texas and its long line of leaders. After commissioning architectural restoration by Dallas firm Burson, Hendricks & Walls and redesigned landscape lighting by John Watson, Governor and Mrs. Clements turned to the private sector for the interior furnishings. Friends of the Governor's Mansion, a non-profit organization chartered in 1979 with an 18-member board, sought the advice of several experts in preserving the Greek Revival grace and cultural significance of the landmark: Foremost among them, Dallas designers Jed Mace and Tom Sellman coordinated colors, accessories, documentary fabrics and floorcoverings, while David Warren, associate director of the Museum of Fine Arts in Houston and former curator of Bayou Bend, was an essential advisor in amassing museum-quality 19th-century American and Texas antique furnishings to augment the existing Mansion collection. Today, flawlessly authentic, the Mansion is the embodiment of Texas style both past and present.

After three years' extensive labor, the suite of public rooms recreates the dignity of the 1850s without a trace of their mustiness. From the garden colors to the lustrous fabrics to the uplifting patterns that weave their magic throughout the house, the Mansion is welcoming in an utterly contemporary way.

To duplicate the sort of non-purist collection that might have once populated the Mansion's rooms, furnishings—largely American Empire—also include some excellent late Federal and early Victorian examples. Cabinetmakers represented are of the upper eschelons: Duncan Phyfe, Joseph Barry, Charles-Honoré Lannuier, Mallard and Belter among them. Many of the fine pieces were handed down by past governors; one such treasure—a hammered tin grandfather clock owned by the Pease family—is thought to be the single remaining original appointment.

Repaired wide pine floors are exposed around area rugs—either antique Oriental or American-made reproductions inspired by old Aubusson and Savonnerie patterns. In upholstery and curtains, the latter swagged and fringed, silks, velvets and jaspés imitate the 1850s.

Porcelains such as Derby, Coalport, Old Paris, Worcester and Barr and Barr adorn tabletops, mantels and display cabinets with their gently muted colors and patterns. Proud history makes itself known through paintings of the governors and their contemporaries, as well as in period masterpieces documenting events of the day: The enormous Robert Onderdonk oil, "The Fall of the Alamo," is a heart-stopping entrée in the foyer.

For the first time, the Mansion can accommodate more than one overnight guest: The former Sam Houston room featuring the famous Houston bed was moved to the front of the house to make room for the new Pease bedroom, a cherished project of the Clements. In honor of Elisha Pease, the first governor to inhabit the Mansion, the bedroom that now bears his name is furnished with marvelous family heirlooms and memorabilia.

Designing the Governor's Mansion was not unlike working with a stage set, according to Mace. "It's a historical museum, after all. You've got to create a sense of theater for the visitor at the front door," he says, "just like the curtain going up." But the task of simultaneously imbuing that very public place with a feeling of warmth and home is no mean feat. "Even though the Mansion is open five days a week," agrees Mrs. Clements, "it's nonetheless a home for us and for all Texans."

ABOVE: Completed in 1856, the Governor's Mansion was designed in the Greek Revival style with 19-foot Ionic columns and a two-story balustraded portico. As the fourth oldest governor's residence in the country, the Mansion was awarded a medallion by the Texas Historical Commission and is listed in the National Register of Historic Places.

RIGHT: In the small parlor, an 1815 Philadelphia scrolled sofa and mahogany upholstered klismos chairs, c. 1830, join an 1810 Boston card table to create an authentically appointed American Empire salon with Federal touches. Swagged curtains and upholstery in documentary silks are in Empire green and gold tones. Purchased during the Dolph Briscoe Administration, the Osler chandelier was crafted for an Indian sultan.

OPPOSITE: A restful extension of the small parlor, the large parlor is used for both grand- and small-scale entertaining today just as it was in its early years. In both rooms, American rugs duplicate beautiful antique patterns taken from Aubussons and Savonneries. A silver tea service set up on a Boston Empire card table figures among numerous priceless accessories that distinguish the room; of particular interest is a set of Worcester urns (on the mantel) procured from Kensington Palace. The 19th-century portrait is of Governor Richard Coke.
ABOVE: One of the most important furnishings in the house is the Charles-Honoré Lannuier table behind the sofa in the large parlor. From nearly any seat, a view of the small parlor's portrait of Sam Houston as a dashing young man is a stirring historical reminder of the glory of Texas' early days.

ABOVE: Although the goal in furnishing the Mansion was to select uniquely American pieces, a few English examples have yet to be replaced. One, a magnificent dining table brought to the Mansion by Miss Ima Hogg, dominates the state dining room. The royal blue color scheme that originates in a Tabriz rug is a rich backdrop for bright flowers arranged in the Victorian tradition and a seven-piece Irish crystal garniture. Old Paris porcelains and a Paul Storr wine cooler adorn the mantel.

OPPOSITE: Against full-length glass curtains, opulent valances swagged in the manner of the period admit sunlight in the conservatory. An Empire sofa and wing and tub chairs complement a drop-leaf and two end tables attributed to Duncan Phyfe; the Sheffield epergne is part of the Mansion collection.

ABOVE: Designed to create a stunning—if restrained—first impression, the foyer's fine Persian rugs and Empire furnishings take a back seat to Robert Onderdonk's 19th-century oil, "The Fall of The Alamo." In addition to the Osler chandelier, 1820 astral lamps illuminate the whole space with a nostalgic glow.

OPPOSITE: One of the coziest rooms in the house, the library—formerly the office for the governor-in-residence—was the site of many of Texas' most historical decisions. Its restoration therefore centers around commemoration of past governors; the Empire sofa is from the descendants of Governor Elisha Pease, while gentleman's chairs were given by the family of James Allred. Hardware tiebacks featuring the Lone Star of Texas are a modern-day tribute in concert with vintage memorabilia like the daguerreotype of Sam Houston's flamboyant signature.

LEFT: The Sam Houston bedroom was moved to the front of the house to make way for a second bedroom dedicated to Elisha Pease, the first governor to take up residence in the Mansion. Custom-designed fabric patterned after Texian Campaign china is a regal companion to the famous Sam Houston bed, believed to have first appeared in the Mansion in 1859. The well-known portrait of Houston is joined by an exquisite bust by Elizabet Ney.

ABOVE: Open to the public for the first time as a cherished project of Gov. and Mrs. William P. Clements, Jr., the Pease bedroom is furnished with family heirlooms; the tester beds were retrieved from the archives, while the desk was located in the Capitol. Thought to be the only antique present at the completion of the Mansion in 1856, a tallcase clock of hammered tin is still greatly admired and fondly remembered by the Pease family. Special handwoven friendship quilts feature the Mansion itself as well as Texas wild flowers, the mockingbird, the Texas Seal and various state luminaries.

ARTISTIC DESIGNS: A MARRIAGE OF DIVERGENT STYLES

About the same time that celebrated architect Philip Johnson was in the throes of his acclaimed glass house in Connecticut, he also was designing his first residential project in Houston. A stark, flat-roofed structure, it bore most of the Johnson trademarks of the day; some 30 years ago, clean Miesian lines, an abundance of glass and a lack of surface ornamentation constituted rather revolutionary departures from the graceful homogeneity of Houston's traditional residential districts.

No doubt, in Johnson's mind, the house was conceived as the picture-perfect setting for a few strategically placed Barcelona chairs, a teak Aalto table or two and perhaps some unobtrusive recessed lighting, all against severely laundered white-on-white. Not so, however, for the owner, whose artistic tastes embrace the gamut of periods, moods and genres.

If modern architecture and colorful interiors form two opposing sides of the triangle, one of the country's most compelling private art collections provides the base that completes the figure. American and European modern art, African sculpture and bibelots from across the globe are neither overwhelmed by foolish virtuoso architecture nor sterilized by white walls and marble floors. Instead, the three elements—architecture, interior and art—are gleefully fused into an unforgettable setting for family, friends and visitors.

The owner has five children, but she was not enthralled with the notion of an unwieldy, rambling structure that might demand an inordinate amount of maintenance. "I had very precise requisites for the house," she says, and in spite of Johnson's established commitment to International Style, he was able to satisfy all his client's needs while creating a design in keeping with his own firm aesthetic convictions.

"I wanted one large space for entertaining," says the owner, "and I wanted the children to have their own wing with direct access to the kitchen." Accordingly, on one side of an impressive glass-walled living room banked by a lush backyard full of dramatic modern sculpture and a walled atrium filled with flourishing tropical plants, the master suite is balanced by a series of children's rooms.

Once installed in the house, the owner elected to have her couturier, Charles James, draft all the interiors. "He was a friend. I admired his genius," she says of the American dress designer, whose heyday in the '40s and '50s was filled with important commissions from actresses of both stage and screen. James typically drew upon the finest, most luxurious goods for his very regal, feminine fashions.

Treating the entire house as a blank canvas, James the couturier became James the artist, applying his own japanned colors in an impressionistic manner that ranged from the surrealism of actual faux bois and cloudy gouache-like pastels to opaque slates and luminescent topazes. What he didn't paint, he might cover with a fuschia felt or a deep rose velvet; in lieu of a door he often hung heavy velvet curtains acutely reminiscent of lofty theater sets.

The tiniest niches and most unassuming corners were given unprecedented dignity via rich polychrome surfaces, gilt and brass trim and lovely flowing volumes. The large living room seems open and airy; its glass walls usher in panoramic views on either side, and its black Mexican tile floors are punctuated occasionally by a bright rug.

Remarkably ahead of their time, James' furniture designs evoke images of his beautiful, sensuous fashions. The same undulating effects here shape shelves and countertops, as well as a sinuous sofa in the dining room and a rippling loveseat in the living room.

The unexpectedly comfortable concoction that results from straight lines versus curved, glass versus velvet and neutrals versus dazzling color creates an environment at once fascinating and relaxing that, despite its mind-boggling worth, is never pedantic. In fact, the ambiance is delightfully reminiscent of the unintimidating rooms of Paris' *Musée Jeu de Paume*, its walls literally brimming with priceless works that the viewer longs to reach out and touch.

LEFT: In the welcoming entry, a beautiful Max Ernst dominates the sweeping wall space above an unusually long Belter-style sofa. Other antique Belter-style furnishings, more restrained than the master ebeniste's *flamboyant Victorian pieces, congregate alongside a life-sized lion sculpture by Felipe Archuleta and a smaller piece by Eduardo Chillida.*

ABOVE: A serene fusion of brick and black Mexican tile, the central nave that transects the entry is yet another gallery of fine artwork. Surreal paintings by Louis Fernandez echo the tranquil slate tones throughout the corridor. In the foreground, unique round sculptures are by Takis.

ABOVE: *Hidden in a corner of the living room, even a tiny bar reflects the sensuous touch of American couturier Charles James, who designed the house's interiors. Amid rows of tinted glassware and unusual decanters, a plethora of miniature drawings by such luminaries as Claes Oldenburg, Franz Kline and Pablo Picasso delight the eye.*
OPPOSITE: *Creating a lovely vignette in the entry, two 19th-century leather chairs treated in the Belter manner flank a sculpture by Brauner.*

ABOVE: The broadly eclectic tastes of the owner are particularly manifest in the open living room. Against architect Philip Johnson's clean, rectilinear backdrop, she has amassed furnishings of every period—from High Victorian to art deco to contemporary—and accessories of every description. The extraordinary result juxtaposes a Magritte painting with a vintage grand piano and a stone Egypto-Roman funerary mask with an antique Italian angel.
OPPOSITE: Framed against a natural mural formed by tropical plantings are a Colima statue, a Nigerian piece crafted by the Yoruba and a Dogon figure from Mali. Dramatic in both scope and shape, the nearly floor-to-ceiling snake headdress is from West Africa.

OPPOSITE: Custom-designed by Charles James, the sinuous curves of a magnificent modular sofa form a unique seating area in a corner of the large living room, which is effectively landscaped into three such conversation-provoking nooks to streamline the space for entertaining. ABOVE: A bronze rooster from the African Benin culture is simply placed next to a Roman bowl to create a lovely, uncomplicated still life. One of several handsome garden sculptures, a Max Ernst work dominates the view from the living room.

LEFT: The dining room is a comfortable setting where reflection and relaxation are as frequent a pastime as savoring delicious meals. To delight the visual sense as well as the palate, the room is enveloped by the master paintings of Archambault, Wifredo Lam, René Magritte and Yves Tanguy. *ABOVE: Among the dining room's pivotal furnishings are a rangy suede-covered sofa by Charles James and a one-of-a-kind lacquered chest covered in period tobacco- and cigar-box wrappers. Muted colors provide an effective showcase for people and art alike.*

A HISTORIC KING RANCH HOME RESTORED

In the late 1800s, Captain Richard King owned a good part of South Texas. His expanse of land was so vast that the portion that remains today still constitutes the largest privately held ranch in the United States. At that time, cattle from the King Ranch and neighboring herds had to be driven hundreds of miles north to railheads in Kansas. To rest and water the stock for the long journey, ranchers brought their cattle to La Puerta de Agua Dulce ("Gateway to Sweet Water"), a section of Richard King's ranch with abundant water and pasture.

When Captain King's son, Richard, married in 1882, the elder King and his wife, Henrietta, built a house at La Puerta and gave it to their son and his bride as a wedding present, along with 46,000 acres of land and use of the original King Ranch brand, the HK. The King Ranch then took to branding their cattle with the running W.

La Puerta burned in 1901 but was rebuilt in 1904, this time with the kitchen and dining room in a separate building. The home stayed in the King family until 1974, when Belton Kleberg Johnson, a direct descendant of Captain Richard King, purchased it from the Kings. Today, La Puerta de Agua Dulce is a 10,000-acre working ranch with 450 purebred Santa Gertrudis and 5,300 acres of milo maize and other crops. The two-story white frame building is rimmed by palm trees and a fence to keep the cattle outside. A long second-floor veranda catches the gulf breezes. The total effect is one of warmth blended with simple dignity; the house is both a home and the headquarters of a busy ranch.

But things weren't always that way. Before the Johnsons bought La Puerta, the 6,100-square-foot house stood unoccupied for 50 years and was in considerable need of both restoration and the addition of such modern conveniences as kitchen appliances and central air conditioning and heating systems. The restoration and updating presented an unusual challenge for Mrs. Johnson and San Antonio interior designer Tilford Collins.

The design of the house was quite modern for the turn of the century. The home included four large bathrooms and a number of large trunk closets—so called because of their size, which rivals that of many modern dressing rooms. La Puerta also had its own carbide plant, which fueled the delicate gas chandeliers in the living room and parlor and the lights on the newel posts at the foot of the main staircase. Collins had all the gas fixtures wired for electricity but otherwise kept them the same. The most unusual light is the antler chandelier at the head of the staircase, made out of a collection of horns from bucks bagged by Johnson's son, Kley.

In restoring the house, Collins made few basic structural changes, but he did bring the kitchen and dining room back inside. The new dining room is warm and inviting, only slightly more formal than the rest of the house. Candelabra that once belonged to Mrs. Johnson's grandmother grace one wall. When guests visit the ranch, Mrs. Johnson likes to decorate the table with a centerpiece of giant zinnias. "They're the only flowers I'll have here," she says. "Nothing else seems appropriate."

Most of the furniture in the house once belonged to Mr. and Mrs. Richard King II. While the downstairs rooms seem well suited to the day-to-day business of ranch life, the upstairs is a more intimate and private retreat. The open sitting room at the head of the stairs contains a horn tête-à-tête that once belonged to fashion designer Halston as well as wicker furniture that was found in the attic and restored. The breezy wide veranda provides more upstairs living space, as well as a perfect place to glide gently back and forth on an old-fashioned porch swing and survey the surrounding countryside.

There's a fine sense of place to La Puerta de Agua Dulce, a sense of noble past preserved. The same vital spirit and unabashed honesty that made the King Ranch a legend live on at La Puerta today.

FAR LEFT: *Much of the upholstered furniture in the living room is covered with hides from the Johnson cattle. Chandeliers and newel post lights are original gas fixtures wired for electricity.*

LEFT: *Warm tones used in the dining room are in keeping with the period without being too formal.*

BELOW: *The tiles that form the front of the living room fireplace incorporate the name of the ranch and the original King Ranch brand. Flora and fauna painted on the tiles are indigenous to South Texas.*

ABOVE: The long veranda offers a shady place from which to survey the seemingly endless landscape and watch the clouds roll in from the gulf.
RIGHT: La Puerta de Agua Dulce ("Gateway to Sweet Water") stands with functional dignity, the headquarters of a successful ranch in South Texas. The two-story white frame building is rimmed by palm trees and a fence to keep the cattle outside.

LUXURY AND GRANDEUR IN A DISTINCTIVE SALON

Twenty-one stories above the woods and waters of Dallas' Turtle Creek, only the sounds of silence—those private echoes of the mind's ear—speak to Sigmund Mandell. This aerie of tranquil solitude high above the city deserves the respectful reception of a man who has spent the last 40 years cautiously and discerningly amassing the treasured accoutrements of a private world.

The result is an extraordinary departure from the norm of condominium living in the Eighties. In the urbane mold of a Parisian salon, Mandell's home abounds with reminders of other periods and places that are well worth preserving. Stunning English, Italian and French antiques hold revered places in this appreciative atmosphere.

But this is by no means a touch-me-not shrine destined to grow musty with time. "I use everything, I touch everything," explains Mandell. "I like to think that what I have here is a friendly, non-intimidating museum. Every chair is comfortable, and every table can hold a drink."

It didn't happen that way by accident. The furnishings were assembled over the years on 33 trips to Europe as well as on random occasions in Dallas and New York. In each instance, buying for its own sake was never the overriding motivation. Although the furnishings range in origin from Chinese Chippendale and Queen Anne to English Regency and Italian Empire, "I have always tried to keep to one taste, one mood," says Mandell. "I wasn't buying something just to be buying. Each piece had to fit with one another."

All of it came home to the high-rise condominium, long considered one of Dallas' most prestigious addresses, where Mandell has lived since 1958. With the assistance of interior designer Robert L. Koenig, the European furnishings assumed paramount importance in a plan that conveys luxury and grandeur despite the inescapable fact that the one-bedroom condo offers little more than 1,200 square feet of living space. For openers, mirrored walls in both living and dining areas combine with flowing furniture arrangements to create the illusion of greater depth.

The practicality of the design is reflected in the comfortable, gracious style of the owner's frequent at-home entertaining. The manager of a retail department store, Mandell has hosted cocktail parties for up to 40 people.

For more intimate evenings, dinner is served on the round walnut Directoire table with its accompanying eight Italian Louis XVI chairs covered in parrot green Hermès leather. On these occasions Mandell may take advantage of his collections of antique Georgian silver and Rosenthal china.

At other times, the surroundings are simply one man's retreat from the busy world. Explains Mandell, "Do you know that when you go to Versailles, you see something beautiful everywhere you look? Well, in my small way, I have tried to create that same kind of beauty in my lifestyle. I surround myself with it.

"I have a carefree kind of living. In the city, it seems to me that the high rise is the total expression of life, easy and uncomplicated. I like that; it satisfies a lifestyle. But at the same time, it affords me a background of such scale that I can house my collections."

At night, when the distant city lights create a view straight out of fantasy, the Mandell condo seems to remove itself from the present and dissolve into a resplendent past. And like some latter-day time traveler, Mandell sees history through the *camera obscura* of his surroundings. The object of his attention might be, for example, the quiet brilliance of the living room's multi-hued Savonnerie carpet, circa 1820; the eternally fascinating contents (primarily European and Chinese porcelains) of a Chinese Chippendale vitrine, circa 1800; or a pair of terrestrial and celestial Chippendale French-style globes, dated 1780 and unearthed separately nearly a decade apart.

For Mandell the attraction is infinite, impervious to the passage of time and its consequences. "I find being among fine things to be relaxing," he says simply. Borrowing from the graceful past, he finds endless enrichment for the present.

LEFT: The living room, flavored by the elegance of its period furnishings, lends itself to formal entertaining. The round glass-topped coffee table, its base a capital from an antebellum New Orleans home, proves functional as well as decorative.
ABOVE: Louis XV armchairs, upholstered in mocha suede, pose demurely before an English Regency collector's cabinet guarded at its base by a pair of English Regency gilt griffins.

ABOVE: Gloriously reflected in the dining room's mirrored wall are Mandell's collection of Georgian silver, antique Rosenthal service plates and Royal Crown Derby dinner plates.
OPPOSITE: A Chinese K'ang Hsi turquoise lamp on a French rouge marble table banded in bronze finds its counterpoint in a pair of Louis XVI wall sconces.

OPPOSITE: The bedroom provides an elegant backdrop for carefully acquired antiques such as the Savonnerie rug, French Directoire bed, a Louis XVI pedestal bearing a bronze of the Comtesse Madame du Barry and the saber-legged English Regency armchairs.
ABOVE: An assortment of lapis lazuli, jade, silver gilt, malachite and red jasper boxes adorns the Louis XV black-lacquered bureau plat *in one corner of the living room. A Louis XVI converted oil lamp in warmly patined bronze graciously illuminates the 18th-century coromandel screen.*

STAGECOACH INN: COUNTRY QUARTERS RESTORED

On a 19th-century passage from Houston to Austin or Waco, one of the favorite rest stops for travelers, mail couriers and transporters of assorted goods was the Stagecoach Inn at Chappell Hill. A major overnight stop for Texas' first stagecoach line, the Inn, with its beautiful Greek Revival proportions, renowned victuals and comparatively luxurious accommodations, was for many years a warm and welcome sight for weary travelers.

Mary Haller, the granddaughter of pioneer settler Robert Wooding Chappell, bought 100 acres of the fertile land and named the town in 1847. Her husband, Joseph Haller, was the town's first postmaster. In 1850, they built the 14-room Inn to serve the two stagecoach lines throughout the Civil War.

The Greek Revival style of architecture became the predominant architectural mode for the township; the Inn is a quintessential example of the style and the characteristic variations made on it by regional architects. The two-story house, like most of the buildings in Chappell Hill, was constructed of stone and native cedar; the paint, plaster and tin were believed to have been hauled overland from Houston. Typical of the period, the entire framework was mortised, tenoned and pegged.

Fairly pure in style and plan, the Inn breaks from the Greek Revival tradition only in a long rectangular room at the rear, perpendicular to the central entry hall. Usurped from the characteristic hallway, the space was used as an oversized dining room to feed the hotel's many guests. The first floor was composed of a lobby, dining room and bedroom, while the upstairs consisted exclusively of guest rooms, each featuring a washbowl and pitcher—a rare luxury in those primitive parts.

The Federal influence is seen in a central portico that frames the front door in lieu of a full-length, temple-like veranda. Paired Doric columns support a balustraded upper gallery, and a simplified cornice gives rise to a terneplate roof. An exquisite Greek key frieze wraps around the roofline, and unique downspout heads bear the proud Lone Star of Texas with the date 1851, the year they were added to the house.

Years of neglect in the following century led to utter abandonment and attrition of the once gracious hostel. The general consensus was that the Inn should be razed, much to the anguish of the Chappell Hill populace, who remembered it as the bulwark of a thriving yet vanished heyday. In 1976, however, the Inn was purchased and restored by Houston architect Harvin Moore and his wife, Elizabeth. It now stands on the corner of Main and Chestnut streets as a proud remnant of the days of the Texas Republic, once again an exquisite pillar of a quiet Texas village.

Despite the lamentable state of the Inn when they purchased it, the Moores, who already had renovated several German cottages in Round Top, recognized its historic and architectural value. After researching the Inn's history, the couple set about restoring its former grandeur with authenticity and practicality.

Keeping the original floor plan intact, the Moores made only minor changes in the name of convenience: A former pantry is now the kitchen, the old lobby is now the dining room and the immense hotel dining room has become a spacious keeping room. Beautiful museum-quality antiques collected in Europe, New England and Texas harmoniously populate the rooms alongside elegant Oriental, hooked and braided rugs and American primitive paintings. "If there's any particular point to stress," explains Mrs. Moore, "it's the fact that the Inn is not a historical museum. It's a home for us, our children and grandchildren."

The reaction of the people of Chappell Hill to the astonishing restoration of the Stagecoach Inn has been positive since its inception. "That's perhaps the most rewarding aspect of all," Mrs. Moore says. "It's something they've wanted to do for years, and to see it brought back to life after so long is a thrilling sensation."

LEFT: Without jarring the historical mood of the room, a contemporary sofa covered in a chintz pattern faces two Chippendale chairs upholstered in crewelwork. Used as a coffee table, the black stagecoach box, c. 1858, seems the perfect accompaniment to the reproduction of Remington's "The Old Stagecoach of the Plains" hanging over the mantel.
ABOVE: One of Texas' outstanding examples of early Greek Revival architecture, the Stagecoach Inn was built in 1850.

ABOVE: In the dining room, the Texas corner cabinet, dated 1870, displays English china.
OPPOSITE: French Provincial dining room table and chairs are imaginatively paired with a Fayette County curly pine cupboard, a handwoven ingrain American rug and an American primitive painting.

RIGHT: An 1830 wagon seat in the upstairs hall was once used to accommodate ladies and children on rough rides.
BELOW: With a dresser to match, the Eastlake bed is accented by a signed Pennsylvania coverlet, 1839.
OPPOSITE: In the upstairs sitting room, an oak Biedermeier daybed with a handwoven antique coverlet sits on a rug braided by Mrs. Moore.

OPPOSITE: Made in Ammonsville, Texas, the curly pine wardrobe toured with the Boston Museum of Fine Arts' Far West exhibit. At the foot of the Eastlake bed, the "Kissing Doves" quilt is part of a special antique collection. ABOVE: Dated in 1853, the S.H. Granger primitive hangs above a four-poster rope bed with a coverlet in the "Wild Turkey" pattern.

URBAN OUTLOOK IN A SUBURBAN SETTING

One of the special plusses that seems to come as an inherent bonus with all large houses is the singular freedom that results from an abundance of space: space to move around without constraint, space that lets in the light of sky and landscape and opens wide the field of possible interior design. But expectedly, there exists a potentially frightening flipside as well: Space must be reckoned with, and reckoned with well. Poorly orchestrated, whether in scale or layout, it becomes the worst sort of domestic nightmare.

One particularly magnificent structure, set grandly amidst the verdant prairie of North Dallas, happily combines the talents of Midland architect Frank Welch and Fort Worth designer David Corley to create a perfect setting for civic entertaining and for showcasing a prized collection of Southwestern art. The resultant size and design make the home ideal for business magnate Philip Jonsson.

A brilliant symphony of glass and whitewashed stucco, the compelling layout integrates the gargantuan Texas outdoors in a square floor plan encircling an open atrium where a bubbling fountain plays. Corley, of the design firm Minton-Corley, fused varying scales and volumes and deftly fine-tuned both light and color to bring the massive rooms into comfortable proportion. Drama was retained, yet not at the expense of the reassuring humanity that might have been lost in an exclusively contemporary decorative scheme.

"Besides the clean contemporary lines of the architecture," explains Corley, "the strongest directive is the exterior; it's impossible to ignore the outdoors in this house. There's a lot of glass, a lot of height and a lot of light." Corley therefore elected to paint walls common with exterior walls the same white tone so as not to lessen their architectural integrity. Interior walls are beautifully softened by taupe limousine cloth and complemented at regular intervals by Italian wool carpeting in the same subtle shade. Strongly patterned Mexican onyx floors are frequently left bare, while color floods the palette via bright artwork and rich Oriental rugs.

The immensity of the rooms—which are rendered even more sweeping by the lush vistas so integral to the design—is treated handsomely with a blend of contemporary and antique furnishings, all on a massive scale. Comfortable and soft, the modern designs reinforce spare, straightforward architectural lines. European 15th- and 16th-century antiques were chosen expressly for their heavy, masculine contours and the dark, rich woods that contrast so effectively with the white exterior walls and neutral interior tones. They soften the angularity while concurrently adding detail and history to the entire setting.

Throughout the house, bright, assertive artwork comes forward as neutral background colors recede, and a vast collection of American Indian folk art brings the natural flavor of the Southwest to a house whose architecture is synonymous with that region's legendary wide-open spaces.

Flow from room to room, without question one of the most essential ingredients of fine interior design, is perhaps never so important as in a house that enjoys an abundance of large-scale civic entertaining. Soaring architectural space, of course, is a necessity, but that alone will not provide a realistic solution to the inherent problems of a house that must be a home as well as a showplace. No matter how many benefit dinners are planned for 300, there will be an equal number of cocktails for three, and the three must be as cozy as the 300 are uncongested.

The natural placement of furnishings and use of open spaces developed by Corley adapts the design effortlessly to the broad variety of gala occasions Jonsson hosts.

"I particularly liked the house's being large and simple—free of gingerbread," says Jonsson. "I felt the furniture should conform in its massiveness, but I didn't want it to be stark. Even the contemporary pieces are classic, and the antiques and collections have interesting visual detail."

LEFT: Encircling a custom coffee table made of five slabs of Texas fossil stone topped with glass, massive contemporary seating covered in the same limousine cloth as the walls suits the enormous scale of the living room. Natural flow into the dining room easily accommodates large parties.
ABOVE: A vivid Bert Phillips oil hangs above a 16th-century Florentine walnut credenza, one of a collection of Renaissance-era pieces throughout the house.

OPPOSITE: *Above an onyx-topped sideboard, a Julio Larraz oil brings bright colors to the dining room in a fresh echo of outdoors.* ABOVE: *Atop an antique Heriz of exceptional color and design, a superb 13-foot oak Flemish refectory table is dated c. 1580-1600. The chairs are covered in water buffalo hide. A 1650 Italian walnut cabinet holds an 1875 English carved architect's model.*

In a son's bedroom, early 19th-century Mexican ceremonial masks from the state of Guerrero are of colorfully painted wood and hang above a 1650 Spanish cabinet. Above the beds, masks of hammered copper set a masculine tempo for the rest of the room.

In the family room, a late 17th-century Portuguese walnut settee is stationed in front of shelving that displays fine examples of American Indian basketry and ceramics from around the turn of the century. The creeping terra-cotta fox, c. 1900, was made in France.

ABOVE: A magical illusion of mirrors, marble and outdoor greenery, the master bath is a wonderful haven distinguished by African primitive art. On the back of the tub, a Bambara warrior and horse from Mali accentuates the spirit of kurumba antelope heads, used in a tribal dance ceremony in the Tribiali region of Mali.

RIGHT: An arresting Mondrianesque palette in the master bedroom is enhanced by the masculine lines of a black lacquered tree-trunk bed and hand-carved, branch-like Italian bedside tables. A dramatic Fritz Scholder painting dominates the private domain.

THE CLASSIC HARMONY OF RIVER OAKS

Master architect John Staub employed all his considerable talents when he designed this gracious art deco-influenced mansion more than 45 years ago. Set amid formal gardens, the River Oaks classic was built in a "T" shape to create attractive interior sight lines. Doorways and windows frame each other from one room to the next. And although spacious, the rooms are so well proportioned they never seem intimidating.

The H.R. Cullen family, founders of Quintana Oil, commissioned Staub to design the two-story stone house and spared no expense in its construction. The impressive stairway is a graceful reverse-S curve distinguished by a balustrade of pewter foliage and Steuben glass fleur-de-lis. The domed ceiling over the stairwell is embossed with a bas-relief Greek key and palm design. White and slate grey Italian marble shot with veins of *rouge royal* tile the entry hall and gallery, while the other floors are teak and mahogany. The chandeliers are Waterford crystal, the sconces Waterford and Wedgwood. The Cullens enjoyed this extravagantly appointed home until the late 1950s when, their children grown, they sold the house for a smaller residence.

After remaining vacant for eight years, the proud structure was acquired by another prominent Houston family. Oscar Wyatt, Jr., founder and chairman of the Coastal Corporation, and his wife, Lynn Sakowitz Wyatt, bought the mansion in 1965 and began refurbishing it. Again, the owners spared no expense.

Instead of altering the design of the house, the Wyatts focused their efforts on decorating it in a light and airy French manner that was not too formal, yet reflected their international lifestyle. Under the guidance of Dallas interior designer John Astin Perkins, Mrs. Wyatt created the imaginative design scheme. In just five days, they had chosen the major pieces of furniture, fabrics, wall colors and rug patterns. Most of the furnishings are Louis XV and Louis XVI, accented by a few English pieces and quality reproductions. Perkins selected four or five pieces for Mrs. Wyatt to choose from, relying on the sense of color and proportion evident in her own Fauvist-inspired paintings displayed throughout the house. The tasteful decorating scheme consistently accents rather than upstages Staub's architecture. "I thought the house had such an exceptional architectural balance," explains Mrs. Wyatt, "I didn't want the furnishings to detract from it."

Over the years, the Wyatts have modified the decor slightly. Paintings and craft collections are arranged throughout the house. Among the groupings are Chinese snuff bottles, miniature French clocks, photographs of celebrity friends in unusual frames and boxes made of extraordinary materials such as staghorn and porcupine quills.

While the exquisite decor blends with Staub's classic design to make the River Oaks mansion a showplace, the Wyatts' active lifestyle and lavish entertaining bring their home to life. Whether the evening calls for an intimate dinner for eight in the wine cellar or a gathering for dozens in the dining room, the Wyatts do it with flair. The finest crystal, china, linens and cuisine are proffered in an atmosphere of grandeur.

While meeting the demands of large, extravagant parties, the mansion's serene elegance provides its owners with a restful retreat from business pressures and social commitments. Done in lovely Wedgwood blue and ivory, the master suite especially provides a quiet haven for relaxation.

Although the suite is decorated with formal curtains, Wedgwood sconces and crystal chandeliers, it has been made warmer with homey touches such as paintings by Mrs. Wyatt, quilts and other personal treasures.

"So often you walk into a room and immediately sense that untouchable feeling," says Mrs. Wyatt. "We didn't want that at all. I didn't want to overdo it with furnishings or accessories. I like a comfortable, lived-in feeling that also exudes elegance."

LEFT: In the drawing room, the painting over the fireplace is by French Impressionist Voltat. The settee on the right is a signed Louis XV. The hassock is Louis XV and has retained its original needlepoint.
ABOVE: A Texas classic, the Wyatt house was designed by Houston architect John Staub, whose stamp of genius marks the development of River Oaks.

ABOVE: The mirror in the formal English dining room was custom made to fit above the Louis XVI side table, which supports two Oriental urns.
OPPOSITE: Six of the dining room chairs are antiques; the others are reproductions by Frederick Victoria of New York. The table is set with Waterford crystal and Royal Crown Derby china, c. 1740.

OPPOSITE: *A signed Louis XV desk in the library showcases a staghorn box, a porcupine quill box and photographs of famous friends. The charcoal portrait of Mrs. Wyatt is by French artist Jean Tabaud.*
ABOVE: *The house was designed so that doorways and windows frame each other from room to room.*

LEFT: Exquisite French furnishings and Wedgwood accents combine with Mrs. Wyatt's own Fauvist-inspired paintings and extraordinary collections to create a sumptuous boudoir.
ABOVE: The writing table in the bedroom is a kidney-shaped Louis XV desk topped with tooled leather.

GRANDE DAME OF THE GULF

During the last quarter of the 19th century, Galveston had the distinction of being Texas' "Queen City." As the chief port on the Gulf of Mexico and a center of commerce in the South, the island city's title was well deserved. And as Galveston grew and prospered, its citizens flaunted their affluence by erecting homes and commercial buildings that reflected the period's grand and highly ornamented style.

Nicholas J. Clayton, the first professional architect in Texas, designed many of the landmark buildings in Galveston during this era and influenced the planning of many others.

One merchant during Galveston's Golden Age, Jacob Sonnentheil, is believed to have employed Clayton to design his lavish Gothic Revival home. Although the house has never been positively attributed to Clayton, a board uncovered during a recent restoration bears the legend "1887 Ducie." Since Colonel Daniel W. Ducie was Clayton's general superintendent for many years and also designed the interiors of many of his buildings, the Sonnentheil house is almost certainly Clayton's creation.

Whether actually designed by Clayton or not, the house is an outstanding example of architecture in the late 1880s. It represents a successful attempt to translate the grandeur of the expensive stone Gothic Revival style into durable but less expensive cypress, or "carpenter Gothic." The intricate latticework which graces the exterior is a tribute to Ducie and his craftsmen. Below the Ionic capitals of the second-story porch are carved heads, each representing a different European nationality, which were made in Italy especially for the building.

Besides its exquisite carpentry, the Sonnentheil house also is important for its departure from the traditional architectural philosophy of the 19th century, which held that a building's exterior design should dictate the interior space. The Sonnentheil house was planned instead from the inside out. The second floor is an exact duplicate of the first, except that the ceilings on the second floor are 12 feet high whereas those on the first floor are 14 feet.

It is rumored that the expense of construction drove the owner into bankruptcy. Nevertheless, he continued living there until 1911 when he sold it to Judge Charles Stubbs and moved to New York. The Sonnentheil house has since changed owners several times, most recently in 1976 when it was sold to Lee and Marjorie Trentham, who for a number of years had dreamed of owning the home. The Trenthams felt strongly about preserving the architectural heritage of the Victorian showplace and have painstakingly restored the house to its former splendor. They collect Oriental rugs, rare dolls and other antiques, interests that made the prospect of restoring the home particularly attractive to them. The work took more than a year, with an average of 10 to 12 craftsmen and Mrs. Trentham working full time.

The interior was furnished with period pieces and decorated in colors to highlight the hues of the couple's Oriental rugs. Even the landscaping was done with an eye to authentic detail: The shrubs are among those popular in the Victorian era—nandina, oleander and sago palms.

Restoring the Sonnentheil house was a long and complicated task, but the work has not gone unnoticed even in a community full of lovely restored homes. Mrs. Trentham says several people come by every day to gape at the house, and she has constant requests to show it. Some historic home buffs even bring paint chips, trying to match the delicate yellow-beige of the exterior. "I'd always wanted to restore and live in an old home," Lee Trentham says, "and I hadn't seen a house anywhere with prettier carpentry work—gaudy Victorian, if you will. Also, even though the house was in disrepair, it has all of the original hardware and most of the light fixtures."

The result of their work is a house that recaptures the fanciful, extravagant era when Galveston was Queen of the Gulf and every inch a lady.

1826

OPPOSITE: *The original nine-pane stained glass window measuring 10 feet by 14 feet dominates the stairwell.*
LEFT: *Lee Trentham collects Bye-Lo Baby dolls and displays them in the hall alcove to the left of the stairs.*
BELOW: *In the living room, the light fixture and mantel are original. Each panel of the French screen is a painting by Ernest Galvan dating from the late 1800s.*

RIGHT: Hand-painted wallpaper from France brightens the dining room.
BELOW: A French doll, c. 1892, is reflected in an antique petticoat mirror in the guest bedroom. The bed is American Empire, the chair a mahogany Victorian lady's chair designed to accommodate full skirts and stiff petticoats.
OPPOSITE: Portions of the tin ceiling in the front parlor have been repaired using metal foil impressions of undamaged squares.

COUNTRY MANSE: COMPLEMENT TO CONTEMPORARY ART

Some 40 years ago, on the erstwhile site of the Dallas Polo Club, Clint Murchison, Sr., built a magnificent mansion replete with a regal entry, broad hallways, soaring ceilings and auditorium-sized rooms—a gracious country estate for glamorous entertaining and an extremely comfortable lifestyle. Some time later, his children grown and priorities thus considerably changed, he agreed to swap houses with his son John and daughter-in-law Lupe, then a young couple with school-aged children.

The Murchisons trundled north, delighted by the prospect of overflowing into the rural spaces and soaking up a bit of Texas arcadia. Much to their chagrin, however, they found they had absolutely nowhere near the amount of furniture required to fill the formidable manse. "We had about two chairs and a few beds," Mrs. Murchison recalls. "For the most part, you could just roller skate up and down the halls."

Since the couple was still undecided as to what sort of design directions their new home should take, they began to purchase fine, strong art for the walls, leaving much of the floor space quite bare. "It's amazing to consider this now," Mrs. Murchison explains, "but at that time you could buy excellent contemporary art for much less than you could buy even bad furniture. We just began collecting, got hooked and realized we wanted the art to be the focus of the house. In fact, we never did fill the house with an abundance of furniture because if you've got too much going on with it, it tends to confuse the art and lessen its impact."

Fortunately for the Murchisons, their fulfilling, lifelong love of art began just as contemporary art was coming into its own as a recognized genre. Robert Motherwell, Nancy Graves, Louise Nevelson, Helen Frankenthaler, Kenneth Nolan, Robert Rauschenberg—all were among the young artists who captured the Murchisons' hearts in their early stages of creativity.

Today, Mrs. Murchison rotates and adds to her collection roughly every six months. Many of the brave, daring souls she and her husband began collecting now have revered names that make their masterworks almost priceless; she feels she grew up with them, in a sense, and loves nothing more than adding to her collection the works of today's young maverick artists whose outlooks and creations offer telling portraits of our life and times.

For a house of such massive scope and a collection of such value, both are surprisingly unintimidating. An unassuming blend of modern furnishings and collected antique treasures softens the potential glare of the art as well as the imposing stature of the dwelling. "One thing that's understood," says Mrs. Murchison emphatically, "is that although everything tends to be big, it's very warm. You're not afraid to touch. I have too many grandchildren for that."

Much of the reason for that open warmth is due to the design of the house, a design that, according to the owner, "doesn't really say what it is." Suitable for both the contemporary art and the modern and antique appointments, it seems somehow less rote, less fussy. Despite the grandeur of the surrounding 42 acres, with their blossoming fruit trees and the beckoning French-style allée that leads past a dramatic sculpture pool to the front door, the overall feeling is one of close camaraderie with the lovely landscape, a sincere love of the outdoors rather than an overwhelming desire to impress.

Like the art and the furnishings, most of the various antique and contemporary collectibles were bought without a preplanned blueprint; moreover, they are grouped according to Mrs. Murchison's own aesthetic sense rather than categorically.

"The older pieces I have are things that represent my youth to me," says Mrs. Murchison, "things that mean something, just bric-a-brac. I liked to collect things that involved original thinking and good handcraftsmanship, whether it was a Freideberg chair or an inlaid box."

"I love to use everything," continues the collector. "But I like it all to be represented in the way that does it the most justice. Unfortunately, it has turned out to be something of a disaster just because it takes so much work. For example, I have this Majolica vase that's so beautiful I feel it should always have flowers... but that's a lot of work. It drives me crazy if it's not done right, though, so I work hard all the time."

OPPOSITE: The impressive stairwell of the Murchisons' palatial North Dallas residence is graced by a Helen Frankenthaler oil and a bronze sculpture by Alberto Viani entitled "Nude Seducto." Beautiful marble floors lend an unquestionable air of elegance to the entry, stairwell and transverse hallways.
ABOVE: Leading the eye down a central corridor, Rauschenberg's "New York Bird Calls for Oyvindi Fahlstrom" balances a series of carved wooden heads by Aijiro Wakita. Among the few furnishings in the hallway, two scroll-based, red velvet period chairs were used on the set of the classic film "Gone with the Wind."

LEFT: A subtle Morris Lewis painting sets the downbeat for the living room's khaki color scheme. Surrounding an octagonal chrome and glass cocktail table, custom olive suede-covered chairs sit atop a custom rug bordered in the same leather. Through the door to the entry on the right an eruption of color greets the visitor via "Standing Girl," a Frank Gallo sculpture, and an oil by Dallas artist Charles Aberg. ABOVE: A glowing fire warms the rich spectrum of a Gunter Uecker painting that hangs above the mantel and a John Grillo titled "Tempo at High Noon."

ABOVE: *In the luxurious downstairs powder room, a dramatic antique French banquette draped in silvery satin recreates a glamorous movie-star mood.*

OPPOSITE: *A gift from Mrs. Murchison's father-in-law, the mirror-topped French dining table reflects hand-painted silver Japanese wallpaper, Sheffield candelabra and blossoming orchids. Despite the dining room's innately formal setting, Mrs. Murchison feels no qualms at entertaining there in every possible manner—from holiday dinners to Easter parties for the grandchildren to informal Mexican suppers to elaborate civic galas.*

OPPOSITE: *In a guest bedroom, the drama begins with a Chinese painting surrounded by wood-carved sculptures from Macao. Each intricately crafted Ch'ing Dynasty figure rests on an acrylic platform.*
ABOVE: *Resplendently outfitted in black marble with mother-of-pearl inlay, the master bath features a round tub wrapped in tiny black tiles. Counters are laden with a host of mementos of earlier years as well as more recently purchased collectibles: Cut glass, crystal, silver, Majolica pieces and photographs mingle in pleasant confusion. "I spend so much time in here," says* Mrs. Murchison, *"that I like to be surrounded by all the things I love."*

Snaking its way across the expansive grounds that lead to the house, a magnificent aluminum sculpture by Benni Efrat, an Israeli artist, is one of many awe-inspiring landscape designs that enhance the property. Despite the 400-pound cement blocks that secure each bend in the sculpture, it still undulates gracefully in the winds that sweep the prairies north of Dallas. The Murchisons' example is the only piece of its kind in the United States.

THE LEGACY OF BAYOU BEND

Bayou Bend presents a variegated tableau that is emblematic of the woman who created it. At once flamboyant and stately, it is autobiography expressed in architectural design rather than in words.

Ima Hogg's long life was woven closely into the fabric of Texas history. Her father, James Stephen Hogg, governor of Texas from 1891 to 1895, was the epitome of that uniquely Texan political character: the great commoner who was also a man of great wealth.

Miss Ima, as she was known to most of Houston, became one of the city's first cultural leaders. Beloved for her civic philanthropy, she contributed generously to the arts and charitable causes.

In 1926 Miss Ima decided to have a house built in Houston's River Oaks, her brothers' new subdivision. She chose 14 acres of heavily wooded property at a place where the stream changed direction, and she called the estate Bayou Bend.

She asked John Staub, the young man who had designed some of the most elegant houses around Rice University, to submit plans. The design she accepted was a Classical Revival mansion that brought together elements of a number of famous American houses built during the 18th and 19th centuries.

Inspired by Homewood, a country house built near Baltimore in 1803, Staub divided the 18-room house into three symmetric parts, which not only gave the building an appearance of solidity but also suited the Hoggs' lifestyle. The first floor of the middle section was devoted to common use; the upper floor contained Miss Ima's private suite. The east wing, which connected to the main section through a recessed hall, was conceived as a bachelor apartment for brothers Will and Mike. It contained a sitting room, a tap room, a kitchen and two bedrooms. The west wing housed guest rooms and servants' quarters.

The exterior of the house is stucco, a common facing in mansions along the Gulf Coast. Miss Ima had a passion for pink—bright pink—so instead of leaving the stucco natural or painting it she had Staub mix it with rose quartz obtained from a mineral company in which Will owned stock. The result was a rosy exterior that Staub later admitted he had hoped would mellow into a gentler hue.

Bayou Bend appears both grand and solid. Four chimneys—two at the east side of the central block and two at the west—appear to anchor it to the terraced hillside. Virtually every detail was the result of enthusiastic collaboration between Ima Hogg and John Staub. The collaboration was so close, in fact, that later they were hard pressed to recall who was responsible for what.

Architect and architectural historian Howard Barnstone points out that the house is full of borrowed details. The front door is a copy of the one that graces the Nathaniel Russell house built in Charleston, South Carolina, in 1809. The flooring in the living room and in Miss Ima's sitting room, the mantel in her sitting room and two increments of a paneled wall were salvaged from a demolished house in Salem, Massachusetts. Staub copied the scrolled pediments above the doorways from those at Shirley, an 18th-century Virginia plantation house.

The construction on Bayou Bend began in 1927 and was completed in 1928 at a cost of $217,000. At first, Will Hogg complained that Staub had spent too much time and money on the foundation, but he dropped the subject after Buffalo Bayou overflowed its banks in 1929. Although it flooded the first story, the only damage was a few warped floorboards. After Mike married and moved out in 1929 and Will died in 1930, Staub remodeled the house to make the east wing part of the general living space. He remodeled it again in 1965 to turn it into a museum to display the art and antiques Miss Ima had donated to the Houston Museum of Fine Arts in 1958. Each room was designed as a setting for furniture, paintings and decorative arts from a particular period, ranging from the mid-17th century through 1870 and incorporating primitive country styles as well as some of the most sophisticated and expensive pieces of their day.

In 1966 Miss Ima moved to an apartment, leaving the house and collection to the museum and to the citizens of Texas.

ABOVE: *The Philadelphia Hall exhibits superb furniture crafted at the time of the American Revolution.*
RIGHT: *Adam-style ceiling and door treatments enhance the formal dining room.*
OPPOSITE: *Against a backdrop of hand-painted and gilded wallpaper, a five-piece Chinese export garniture, c. 1800, is displayed atop the dining room mantel. A lyre-shaped epergne and matching candelabra of English silver, c. 1805, underscore the English chandelier, dated about 1800.*

ABOVE: A Kerman rug highlights furniture of the Chippendale period in the drawing room; architecture reflects the neo-Palladian style of the late Georgian era. The needlepoint pole screen beside the fireplace traditionally protected ladies' faces from the heat. Gilbert Stuart painted the Vaughan-style portrait of George Washington. RIGHT: The Chillman Parlor is a showcase for furniture from the French-influenced American Empire period, 1810-1830. Elaborate dolphin shapes form the feet of a New York sofa, c. 1820, and the straight-back chair with a delicate harp-shaped design, c. 1820, is a rare example of its type.

ABOVE: The dark blue paneling of the Massachusetts Room pronounces the simple elegance of that state's Chippendale furniture. Whieldon- and agateware from Staffordshire, England, sit on a tea table in front of a mahogany and maple chair-back settee made in Boston in the late 1700s. The 18th-century easy chair is covered with its original bargello flamestitch.

LEFT: The Belter Parlor honors the inventor of the steam press method of curving wood that gave birth to such flamboyant Victorian furniture as the armchair on the left. A rococo revival tea service made by a Baltimore silversmith sits atop an 1850 ash and rosewood center table.

LEFT: Reflecting the nation's prosperity from sea trade during the Federal period, the music room boasts a wallpaper mural of Turkey by Dufort et LeRoy. The mahogany and pine gaming table is dated 1810.
ABOVE: The Texas Room, paneled entirely in cedar, displays English-crafted pottery made especially for Texas, which spotlights scenes from the war with Mexico

OPPOSITE: The colors of the 19th-century glass in the Pine Room are echoed in a 17th-century English decorative box of beading and stumpwork.
ABOVE: A 1750 mahogany card table in the Queen Anne Sitting Room still boasts its original inlaid crewelwork.
LEFT: The Newport Room is the setting for the simple textural style of Rhode Island Chippendale.

OPPOSITE ABOVE: *The curly maple highboy in the Maple Bedroom is dated 1790. Typical of the era, a stenciled border features the pineapple motif that traditionally symbolizes hospitality.*
OPPOSITE: *Pastels popular during the American Federal period accent an 1800 cabriole sofa and a New Hampshire lolling chair in the Federal Parlor.*
ABOVE: *Fronted by a Boston corner chair, c. 1785, a bombé desk adorns the Chippendale Bedroom. A Staffordshire tea set is dated 1815.*

A SCHOLAR'S RETREAT

The 550-acre Tobin farm sits like a stretch of open Hill Country within the city limits of San Antonio. Surrounded by freeways and residential neighborhoods, the land is a lush, rolling expanse of mellow green meadows where more than 100 Shetland ponies graze. What looks like a series of four spring-fed pools with rough limestone banks actually is a 500-foot-long swimming pool, its river-like current maintained by pumps as it flows along a tree-shaded course.

Fifteen years ago, Robert Tobin, a San Antonio drama scholar, opera enthusiast and collector of paintings, sculpture and rare books, decided to build a home on the meadow above the swimming pool. Because his work with the Santa Fe Opera (which he helped establish and worked with for 20 years) and the New York Metropolitan Opera is so demanding, he wanted a house where he could relax in serene surroundings. He enlisted the help of Houston designer Roger Rasbach, who then was living in San Antonio.

"I showed him photos of Egyptian peasant houses, because I liked their angular quality," says Tobin. "Roger took the idea and softened it. I'd been fascinated by Egypt from the ages of eight to thirteen, after someone took me to a performance of *Aida*," he says. "I was a distinguished Egyptologist."

Working together, Tobin and Rasbach designed a spectacular one-story house with only five rooms: a kitchen, dining room, library, master bedroom and combination studio/guest room.

"Bringing the outside in was Roger's idea," Tobin explains, indicating the sliding glass doors and floor-to-ceiling windows that form one wall of each room. Overhangs create covered patios, extending the living area outdoors while protecting it from direct sunlight.

"The whole concept of the house is a return to earth," comments Tobin. The floor is D'Hanis tile from a town west of San Antonio; interior walls are Austin limestone, and the plantings that surround the house are native to the area.

Originally, the flat roof was a tiled garden set among the trees, but the tiles could not withstand San Antonio's torrential winter rains.

The entrance to the house is a windowless wall, its stark simplicity relieved by massive wooden doors Tobin found in northern Mexico.

The hall serves as a gallery for part of Tobin's art collection, including several paintings by Robert Indiana and Eugene Berman. The front doors open onto the glass hallway with a view of the interior garden. Small cannons, believed to be from Lord Nelson's battleship *Intrepid*, share the space with a sculpture by Mary Callery.

To the left, the hall leads to the kitchen and dining room—which open onto an outdoor cooking and eating area—and onto the library, the focus of the house. Measuring 70 by 35 feet with an 18-foot ceiling, the library houses Tobin's awesome floor-to-ceiling collection of books on art, drama, opera, design and poetry. Tobin says the room is a reproduction of his grandfather's library in Austin, where he spent much of his childhood.

By day, the library is a pleasantly informal work space with simple wooden tables and antique lecterns to hold the massive books. But at night, it takes on an aura of elegance. Tobin uses the house for parties, although he does much of his formal entertaining at his Park Avenue brownstone in New York. The design of the San Antonio home, however, is perfect for large groups. People can move from indoor to outdoor spaces without feeling crowded.

There are paintings everywhere in the Tobin house, even in the master bath and the laundry room. Some are by famous names, others by local artists who have captured Tobin's interest.

This remarkable setting is a delightfully unique home, designed for a person who knew what he wanted and whose vibrant, sophisticated, often whimsical personality permeates every room.

PRECEDING PAGES: *What appears to be a creek running along the Tobin property actually is a 500-foot swimming pool.*
OPPOSITE: *Tobin's library, a copy of a favorite childhood retreat at his grandfather's home, is the focus of the house. Ornate columns from Oaxaca, Mexico, are topped by Mexican baroque gilt capitals.*
ABOVE: *The bronze bust of Beethoven is by Emile-Antoine Bourdelle, and the sculptures on the Mediterranean table are working models from monumental pieces Sol De Witt never completed. A Japanese* carishishi, *or wooden dog, stands guard on a shelf next to a sketch by Edward Gorey.*
FOLLOWING PAGES: *All building materials for the library are native to South and Central Texas, from the slatted wood ceiling and D'Hanis floor tiles to the walls of Austin limestone.*

THE SPIRITED RECREATION OF AN ITALIAN VILLA

"History is my great love," declares Mrs. Elton Hyder. "I have no real favorite period because I love them all. I read about the French Revolution or the czars or Easter Island," she rhapsodizes, "and it frustrates me to death that I can't live through all of them."

If that delicious pipe dream is sadly unattainable, Mrs. Hyder has fully compensated for her mortality by filling a large Italianate mansion in Fort Worth with stunning remnants of all these periods.

In what was originally a palatial Tudor home built in 1916 for Mrs. Ollie Burnett, Mrs. Hyder recreated the spirit of an Italian villa she and her husband had admired. French floors and balconies, porches and balustrades, exquisite molding and a ranging stoa were added, lifting the somewhat claustrophobic atmosphere yet retaining the grotto-like ambiance Mrs. Hyder enjoys. "It *is* a dark house," she admits, "but I like that. When you walk in from the intense heat and light we have here six months of the year, it always feels cool and soothing. Once your eyes adjust, the collections come to life."

Designer John Astin Perkins and later the design firm of Loyd-Paxton, both of Dallas, lent their respective talents to organizing the fantastically varied inventory of valuables into a dramatic yet unintimidating style. After Mrs. Hyder firmly decided against furnishing the house with the English antiques she had inherited—"The house just seemed to need more intricacy than straightforward Queen Anne"—and the Americana she had collected, she began a three-year campaign amassing continental styles. She selected primarily Italian and French gilded pieces plus an arsenal of accessories from every country and period under the sun. "It sort of makes people who love those wonderful clean, modern houses very nervous," she laughs.

"I think people are a little afraid of color these days," she continues. "But really, in this house, we have very high ceilings, lots of windows and space, and the color is very uplifting. It's fun. I enjoy the painted European pieces and the gilded ones, but not so much the really formal ones. The charm of the more casual pieces makes me much happier."

Indeed, there does seem little rhyme or reason to Mrs. Hyder's collecting. The fact is that she faithfully abides by one very elementary rule: "If I like it, I buy it," she explains. "It doesn't have to be the finest of its kind, but it does definitely have to appeal to me in design or color or just spirit."

Thus was born an ever-expanding amalgamation of African art and artifacts, New Guinea sculpture, contemporary American art and Old World masterpieces, Mexican santos and retablos, Russian icons and papier-mâché Easter eggs, early American quilts, Oriental rugs, miniature chairs from various countries, Indian and Afghanistan pillows, French Regency doors, rock crystal, Guatemalan silver, ad infinitum. Corners spill over, walls are obscured, table-, console- and desktops are encrusted with the vast accumulation of objects; even the spaces beneath tables bulge with it. And it dazzles the eye—busily, yes, but also joyfully, with the mesmerizing allure of an Italian oil wherein layer upon layer of rich texture and color create the illusion of a third dimension on the flat canvas.

"I like the idea of displaying collections; it seems to give them much more importance," explains the owner. "If you group several items together, what was just a haphazard bunch of pretty things is suddenly a collection with a key, a meaning."

Despite their rarity and antiquity, all the items are used. Thus they delight as well as offer all the conveniences of strictly functional furniture. The rich tapestry creates a welcoming haven for both casual and formal occasions: weddings, christenings, family reunions, debuts. "I have an old-fashioned belief," says Mrs. Hyder, "that if you have a house you love, you should use it for everything. We always have, and it's made the house unforgettable for us."

ABOVE: A multi-colored Turkish rug warms the welcoming entry, where added architectural details like the hand-carved balusters and exquisite woodwork might otherwise have been overwhelming. On either side of the door, a Mexican religious painting, a Miró lithograph and an octagonally framed Indian tonka pick up golden tones. The 18th-century Venetian chest is one of a pair.
OPPOSITE: At the end of the regal dining room, a 17th-century, silver-threaded religious tapestry hangs above an antique English pine mantel. The lengthy Georgian table is opulently set with antique continental silver goblets, Odiot gilded flatware, golden service plates, 19th-century Viennese plates and vermeil soup bowls.

M
R
H

PRECEDING PAGES: A unique centerpiece is created from three bejeweled crowns and antique French candelabra. Flanking a Russian bishop's mitre are two crowns given to Nicholas and Alexandra as presentation gifts from the Russian regiment.
ABOVE: Oversized architectural details like the mauve and white marble columns bring a larger-than-life grandeur to the many smaller collections featured in the living room. In front of an 18th-century chinoiserie leather screen, a 19th-century French terra-cotta bust provides a pleasant contrast to a hand-carved New Guinea sculpture with shell decorations.
OPPOSITE: The living room mantel, a Louis XV masterpiece, is capped by magnificent candelabra from St. Patrick's Cathedral in Fort Worth. Draped in Hungarian embroidered cloth, a round table holds an assortment of collectibles including Russian bronzes and Persian jeweled boxes.

ABOVE: A lustrous pair of Régence doors beckons the visitor into the library through a small but elegant entry. Originally an outdoor porch, the back wall is travertine; against it, a Régence commode is centered between two African tribal seats.
RIGHT: The soft, filtered light of a large 19th-century French oil over the fireplace dominates the library's decorative scheme. The coffee table is an ornamental showcase for a collection of antique Russian silver cups, a Japanese bronze elephant and various examples of Russian holloware. Displayed on a small stand is the Lord High Chancellor's purse, which holds the royal seal of the King and Queen of England. It was used during the reign of Queen Victoria.

Russian and Greek icons and a pair of Bavarian trophy carvings lead the eye to a painted French Empire sofa in the den. Oriental rugs cover the Saltillo tile floor, which Mrs. Hyder commissioned in a time-honored French pattern. The floor was painted a rich green, left for a year and scraped to produce the antiqued appearance it now has. A pair of Louis XV chairs adds further elegance to the room.

OPPOSITE: *Draped luxuriously in an Indian silk drenched in a rainbow of pastels, the bed in the master suite was custom designed. The Biedermeier bureau holds a collection of antique picture frames filled with family photographs. Echoing the soft tones of the bed, a Salle Werner-Vaughn painting hangs above the bureau; a leather Georgian bench sits at the foot of the bed.*
ABOVE: *A colorful collection of antique Russian papier-mâché Easter eggs figures among the lovely collectibles assembled against the yellow Siena marble in the dressing room. Reflected in the Louis XVI mirror is an especially delightful Spanish santo purchased in the Philippines.*

GRACIOUS GEORGIAN: ENTRANCE TO ELEGANCE

A visitor approaching the handsomely landscaped Georgian residence of Dr. and Mrs. Jack G. McNeill of Beaumont would scarcely believe that interior designer Kelly McNeill once characterized the stately structure as "a very dull basic box."

"It was a plain, uninteresting house when we first saw it, but it just naturally seemed to lend itself to an 18th-century look," explains Mrs. McNeill. "We added 2,000 square feet to it, including the living room, the library and a new entryway, and the limestone quoins we put on the corners gave us a point of departure for the interior architectural details."

Inside, the transformation is even more dramatic. When the McNeills acquired the Beaumont house in 1970, they wanted to showcase their extensive collections of antique furniture, rugs and objets d'art.

With this in mind, the living room was literally built around an enormous hand-carved mantel of English pine: The floor had to be dropped 18 inches to accommodate it. Stripped of numerous layers of paint and stained a natural raw sienna to de-emphasize its bulk, the 18th-century piece serves as an imposing focal point, as well as providing inspiration for custom millwork throughout the house. Rose-tinted walls are a warm, neutral backdrop to the colorful florals of a Lavère Kerman rug, also a consideration in designing the room. "There was so much going on, with the rug and mantel and the mix of prints, that I wanted everything else very simple," says Mrs. McNeill.

In the dining room, the designer found herself facing a similar challenge with a treasured Serapi rug. To show the colorful antique to its best advantage, she selected a pale apricot for the walls, accented by creamy pickled molding patterned after that of the living room mantel; the appropriately formal tone is further enhanced by the Hepplewhite mahogany dining room suite. Eighteenth-century maple wainscoting embellishes the junction of wall and ceiling and is incorporated in a specially designed mantel. Elaborate molded niches display antique Royal Worcester china from Mrs. McNeill's collection.

While remodeling the breakfast area, the McNeills discovered rustic brickwork hidden beneath layers of concrete. To enhance the French Provincial feeling, Mrs. McNeill covered antique English sidechairs of bleached mahogany and unmatched Normandy armchairs in country florals of laminated cotton chintz. The unusual mahogany chandelier is also an English antique, but the glass and bamboo table is unmistakably contemporary.

In the library, antique and modern pieces meld with deceptive ease into a comfortable yet stylish retreat. "I painted the walls in three values of a mushroom tone to enhance the millwork," explains Mrs. McNeill. "It's subtle but effective, and it's a good neutral backdrop for the antique Serapi rug."

Plump contemporary armchairs, upholstered in creamy wool, seem not the least bit out of place flanking a marble-faced mantel crowned with a John Singer Sargent portrait and guarded by an unusual leonine fender. The keystone takes its cue from those on the exterior of the house.

"We've tried to acquire tangible assets that will give us pleasure," she comments. "I want the house to reflect our changing interests, but without that 'don't touch' feeling. I'm not interested in a house that looks like a museum."

The master bedroom perhaps best exemplifies Mrs. McNeill's lighthearted approach and innate sense of style. The mantel was specially built to incorporate its swan-necked pediment, another architectural antique. The English tester bed, Beau Brummel nightstands and Imari lamps are also favorite antiques.

In the sitting area, a Chippendale reproduction loveseat blends comfortably with a Louis XVI armchair and Hepplewhite tea table; a plump traditional ottoman and loveseat complete the elegant mélange.

"The house is constantly evolving," says Mrs. McNeill. "We rarely take anything out, but we're always looking for things to put in."

PRECEDING PAGES: A Chippendale sofa is upholstered in an oversized floral of glazed cotton, which is repeated throughout the living room. Antique English armchairs are covered in damask; "Montclair," by George Inness, graces the impressive mantel. The contemporary cocktail table was deliberately selected because it does not mask the prized rug.
ABOVE: Dining appointments fit for a royal feast gleam beneath a dazzling chandelier of bronze and Baccarat crystal. The 18th-century chairs are covered in a vivid simulated needlepoint.
OPPOSITE: The mahogany table is elegantly appointed with 19th-century Royal Worcester china in the classic "Tree of Life" pattern. "Ann, Widow T. Foun," immortalized by Kit Kat Club protegé Geoffrey Kneller, presides over the scene from above the mantel.

With its quaint brick arches and colorful country chintzes, the breakfast room has a French Provincial feeling leavened by the surprise of a glass and bamboo table. The bleached mahogany sidechairs and unusual mahogany chandelier are English antiques.

A dusty-hued floral chintz is repeated throughout the master bedroom for a beautifully pulled-together feeling. For the pickled-finish antique armchair, Mrs. McNeill selected a classic geometric floral. The lacquered mirror is a Queen Anne reproduction.

CONTEMPORARY OASIS ON THE WINDSWEPT PLAINS

Although the spectacular drama of West Texas' blistered plains and endless horizons coins its own special brand of beauty, there is an unquestionable need to build barriers against its frequent harshness. Committed to a frontier lifestyle, Mr. and Mrs. Clyde Grant still sought to create a hint of the exotic in the midst of Abilene's dusty fabric, a low-maintenance, maximum-security environment that would allow frequent travel. "I was born and bred in this briar patch," laughs Mrs. Grant, "and I really wanted to stay here. We love the drama of the elements, but we needed to be able to control them."

With the combined inspiration of San Angelo architect Jack Meek, Dallas-based landscape architects Boyd & Heiderich and Houston designer Gena Toler, the Grants' townhouse evolved into a consummate answer to their needs within a unique contemporary shell. The center unit of a three-dwelling lot shared by friends, the house is an airy living garden where thoughtful flow belies the relatively small 4,000-square-foot space and where the windswept plains seem far away.

"Clean lines and plain but arresting geometry," says Meek, "respond to surrounding commercial buildings, but the house is really just an abstraction of the adobe concept—straightforward and uncontrived on the outside, energy efficient inside."

"Unlike my other jobs, I really can't take much credit for this house," admits Mrs. Gena Toler, the Grants' daughter. "Everything I know now, I learned at Mother's knee." Together, Mrs. Grant and her daughter strove to create a comfortable elegance where fine antiques, contemporary furnishings and the many collectibles amassed over years of traveling would mingle harmoniously. "I wanted a very lofty feeling," explains Mrs. Grant. "The doors are extremely wide and the ceilings are 20 feet tall. All the spaces flow into one another without the intrusion of barriers. I wanted to be surrounded by all the things I love," she continues, "to sit on them, eat off them and admire them instead of locking them away in rooms I'd rarely go into."

Incorporated effortlessly into the overall scheme of the house, the dining room avoids the menacing trap of becoming wasted space. Warmth, character and graceful suitability, however, imbue the room with its own vivid personality. Surrounded by rich pine millwork and a delicate pastel fabric that takes its cue from an antique Chinese rug in the living room, any seat at the table affords the diner warmth from the fireplace as well as the fragrant tropical humidity of an expansive indoor greenhouse running the width of the home.

Although the Grants' passion is gardening, they found the soil and climate in Abilene rather difficult for horticulture. The magnificent garden room at the nucleus of the house provides a year-round vehicle for indulging their favorite pastime. Inward looking and exotic, the sylvan paradise is a lush Garden of Eden that defies the intemperate outdoors. Says Mrs. Toler, "Abilene is not the prettiest city in the world. So we tried to build a wonderful vista within the confines of the house and complement it with a loose, open wall structure that allows an interior view to go beyond just one room."

The house is heated in winter by solar collectors and two greenhouse stoves; fans circulate cool air in the summer. And despite the jungle of trees and flowering plants, maintenance requires less than three hours a week.

Meek placed the garden at the core of the house, so that whether entering through the front door or through the back, the visitor's immediate impression is one of a peaceful outdoor habitat.

Grant's study and a small, intimate seating area extend the already expansive master suite, while a casual eating area expands the dining room. Flanking a stone-paved woodland garden, both spaces are greenly canopied by three 20-foot ficus trees and joined by a rustic pine bridge. "The whole house," says Dick Heiderich, "swells with the sweet perfume of plants, flowers and rich woods."

ABOVE: In a harmonious blend of contemporary furnishings and collected treasures, the living room is particularly distinguished by a large silk pichvais displayed under glass. Above a Chinese chest, the decorative Moroccan mirror was a gift to the Grants from their daughters. The round end table is covered by an antique handkerchief made of Battenburg lace.
RIGHT: The various soft hues of an antique Chinese rug were the creative inspiration for the color scheme of the living room. A wall of books forms a right angle with floor-to-ceiling glass doors that give open access to the garden room.

OPPOSITE: Beneath an opaline chandelier from Taube, an English Regency table is set with china purchased in Hong Kong. Surrounded by rich pine millwork and a delicate fabric which harmonizes with the antique Chinese rug in the living room, the dining area is easily incorporated into the overall scheme of the house.
ABOVE: Above the pine buffet, a Skilling primitive is flanked by Baccarat candelabra.

ABOVE: Australian tree fern, fragrant cardamom ginger, spathiphyllum, creeping fig, banana trees and a plethora of seasonal flowers fill an expansive indoor greenhouse running the width of the house.
OPPOSITE: In addition to raised and sunken gardens at the front of the house, the garden room is variously filled with such exotics as orchids and bougainvillea.

FUSION OF FORMS: METAPHOR FOR MODERNITY

A well-designed house, says Houston architect Irving Phillips, is a scrapbook of ideas, visions and character, an intimate collection of moods and vignettes. While the architect creates the book's spine, cover and blank pages, the residents themselves must fill the pages with their lives.

A case in point is a sculptural Houston residence set amidst a tumble of greenery on Buffalo Bayou—a clean, distinctive architectural statement that succinctly expresses a complex metaphor of the owners' lives. "The shape of this house takes advantage of its setting to provide a kaleidoscope of interior and exterior views," Phillips says.

A harmonious weaving of textures, levels and geometric forms, the exterior presents to the world a face that is architecturally dynamic, yet uniquely private and, at some angles, even austere. Toward the street, horizontal planes of Mexican brick echo the rustic surroundings and provide a secluded haven behind blank walls. Paradoxically, an entrance of rectangular brick and redwood arches frames the house and beckons toward a serene sculpture garden.

As the bayou wraps around the property, the changed perspective transforms the facade, lending greater informality and openness to the vistas. The repeated rectangle motif, seen in broad windows and walls overlooking a cool green terrace, slides along the bayou into an energetic play of angles, strata and forms at the rear terrace.

Here, the home's strictly horizontal flow is broken: A triangular, second-story deck tilts outward toward the bayou; a redwood cylinder and tall brick chimney follow the vertical lines of the trees; and glass slices of a triangular window point skyward.

The symbolic transition between exterior and interior is accomplished through art, in the 11-foot-tall front door sculpted in iron and glass by Arizona artist Thomas G. Bredlow. Providing a first glimpse into the intricate and highly personal world within the walls Phillips created, the door depicts entwined neo-Gothic motifs individually seen as birds or together as a grotesque face.

The living room is filled with African, pre-Columbian and American Indian pieces. Contemporary furnishings, arranged into intimate seating groups, provide a sleek, smooth foil to the crudeness of the artifacts; tawny brick walls, Mexican fish scale tiles, bright splashes of Willem De Kooning oils and the coppery tones of Oriental rugs create a background of warmth and color.

But the physical core of the residence is a highly sculptural spiral staircase. "From here, the house pinwheels out toward the bayou," says Phillips. "If you spin around at this point, you get a complete view of the structure's angles and images."

From a vantage point at the home's center, suites of bedrooms are visible. All open onto the terrace above the bayou, and all are unique portraits of the personalities inhabiting them. The children's rooms are vivid and contrasting reflections of individual character, one bold and dramatic and the other classically understated.

Lushly green, the master bedroom is a picture of subdued elegance sparked with vivacious touches of art. Its soaring ceilings and walls of windows fill the room with light and airiness, a counterpoint to the deep-toned walls and floors. A small study, accessible by private stairs, overlooks the bedroom and secluded greenhouse. "This is my retreat," says the owner. "I've always wanted a study above the bedroom."

Directly at the top of the spiral staircase, the wedge-shaped guest room is simply appointed as a quiet backdrop for lively folk art and quilts. Like all the rooms, the guest room opens onto the outdoors—in this case, via an upper deck overlooking the bayou.

"When you're in this house, you're not sure you're in Texas," says Phillips. "You could as easily be in Europe or in Canada. But for the owners, the feeling has always been that of returning to an old friend, the right setting for their collections and their lives."

PRECEDING PAGES: Architect Irving Phillips' protectively austere exterior sweeps along Buffalo Bayou into a dramatic interplay of glass and brick planes.
RIGHT: Revealing artistic images comprise the entranceway: a custom-designed iron and glass door and a tranquil reflecting pool.
OPPOSITE: A series of rectangular brick and redwood archways leads to a serene sculpture garden.

ABOVE: *Dominated by an abstract Robert Goodnough painting, the dining room is a mix of colors, cultures and textures. The table, a family heirloom, is surrounded by English reproduction chairs; in primitive contrast, African art is silhouetted in the window.*

RIGHT: *All designs in the sitting room, including the double cylinder coffee table, were custom made. The view surrounding the house is of the lush Houston bayou.*

OPPOSITE: A 19th-century Scandinavian tapestry and a brightly painted carved wooden snake are examples of the owners' distinctive folk art collection.
ABOVE: Clay pipes were used to construct a honeycomb of storage racks in the residence's tiny but inviting wine cellar.

WELCOME

OPPOSITE ABOVE: *Fanciful and bright, a collection of folk art, furniture and quilts enlivens the guest bedroom.* OPPOSITE: *The master bedroom is a study in serenity with a display of contemporary paintings and prints. The handmade French bedspread, leather Bruno chair and ponyskin Corbusier chaise add notes of classic simplicity. The study, accessible by private stairway, features an alabaster sculpture by Austin artist Charles Umlauf.* ABOVE: *Overlooking a geometrical teardrop pool, the residence's back facade exposes all the angles and planes of the house and reflects its interior complexity.*

TREASURES OF A GOLDEN AGE

In 1823 a young pioneer named William McFaddin came to Texas from the East. Ten years later, he moved to what is now the Beaumont area to become one of its first three settlers. He established a homestead and began to farm, but the Texas Revolution took McFaddin away from his land. In return for his valor at the Battle of San Jacinto, the Republic of Texas rewarded him with "a league and a labor," nearly 700 acres of property on the outskirts of the fledgling community of Beaumont, plus additional property elsewhere in Texas.

McFaddin's oldest daughter, Di Averill, and her husband lived with her parents, helping to manage the household and care for guests.

In 1902 Spindletop, the state's first oil well, blew a gusher on McFaddin land. A few years later, the house burned, and Di Averill commissioned Beaumont architect Henry Conrad Mauer to build a new home reflecting the family's rising fortunes.

Mauer was a master of grand turn-of-the-century style. He designed a Classical Revival mansion on an imposing scale, then decorated it like a Viennese wedding cake.

Despite the early date of construction, the McFaddin mansion was equipped with the latest conveniences, including electricity, walk-in closets and six full baths.

Although Di Averill commissioned the house's construction, her stay there was brief. After two months of Christmas season party-giving, she decided the mansion was too large and too difficult to manage. She convinced her younger brother, William P. McFaddin, to trade his somewhat smaller house for hers. After moving in, McFaddin and his family made frequent buying trips to New York and New Orleans to purchase the finest furniture and accessories available.

The interior of the McFaddin house combines the use of heavy, masculine oak and mahogany on many of the walls and beamed ceilings with a feminine use of pastels and elaborate ornamentation. Art nouveau stained glass is abundant, especially on the transoms which, together with folding doors, open the house up to Gulf breezes in the summer. A large sleeping porch on the second floor catches the air from three sides. In the winter, fireplaces in almost every room combine with steam heat to fend off the chill. In an unusual architectural feat, five fireplaces share a single chimney.

To provide them with a front parlor in the elegant French style, the McFaddins hired decorators from Kansas City who designed a room in delicate rose and gold. The parlor walls are decorated with molding and hand-painted garlands of flowers, and as do most of the rooms, it boasts an architecturally rare cove ceiling. With the exception of portraits of family members, surprisingly few paintings hang in the house; pictures would detract from the elaborate wall treatments. Instead, Mamie McFaddin Ward, the McFaddins' daughter and present owner of the house, maintains an extensive collection of statuary, vases and Dresden porcelain figurines.

The library is a quiet retreat, with walls covered in golden oak and Dresden green raw silk. The Oriental rugs were custom made for the room. Cupids and other mythical creatures support a French clock and matching candlesticks that dominate the gracious room from their position on a Vernis Martin marble-topped credenza.

The bedrooms have a French flavor as well. The five rose- and cream-colored bedrooms on the second floor feature carved and painted walls. An elevator is concealed behind an art nouveau glass panel.

Since her husband's death, Mrs. Ward has maintained the house as a faithful example of the turn-of-the-century period. In 1971 the U.S. Department of the Interior listed the McFaddin home on the National Register of Historic Places, and in 1976 it received a Texas Historical Commission Official Historical Medallion. Mrs. Ward has established the mansion and its furnishings as the Mamie McFaddin Ward Foundation to help preserve the history of the period in which it was built—Texas' Golden Age.

LEFT: Azaleas surround the porte cochere at the side of the McFaddin house. The two giant oak trees were planted by William McFaddin more than 100 years ago. ABOVE: The mansion stands amid a full city block of lawn and gardens, one of the state's finest examples of Classical Revival architecture.

ABOVE: The floor of the opulent entry hall is covered with a rich Oriental rug McFaddin's daughter-in-law bought from a traveling Syrian rug dealer.
LEFT: Just inside the leaded glass doors, a crystal chandelier lights the hallway. The grandfather clock came from William McFaddin's original house.
OPPOSITE: The dining room sparkles with the McFaddin silver. Mamie McFaddin Ward still uses the room for formal dinners and for buffets serving up to 200 guests.

LEFT: In the elegant front parlor, the walls are decorated with moldings and hand-painted garlands of flowers. The furniture, fireplace screen and Victrola are all Vernis Martin, a French carved, painted and often gilded style. Two Sèvres vases stand on the mantel.
ABOVE: Dresden porcelain figurines grace a Vernis Martin marble topped table and a bombé curio cabinet in the same French style.

ABOVE: The breakfast room opens onto a stained glass conservatory with its own marble fountain.
OPPOSITE: Like many other rooms in the house, a drawing room adjoining the library combines the use of heavy, masculine woodwork with a feminine use of ornamentation. Especially noteworthy is the unusual cove ceiling.

RIVER OAKS LATIN CLASSIC

When Delores Crabb Mitchell, the daughter of one of Texas' oldest ranching families, decided in the early '30s that she wanted a home for her large double lot in Houston's new River Oaks subdivision, she called architect John Staub. He had designed Miss Ima Hogg's Colonial mansion, Bayou Bend.

The architect's elegant, eclectic style made him a favorite with wealthy Houstonians. Staub designed the first River Oaks Country Club building, and his residential work there has given the tree-shaded neighborhood its distinctive character.

Staub's designs are eclectic as opposed to modern. That is, he picked out forms from the past and put them together to suit contemporary lifestyles. When Mrs. Mitchell requested a Spanish hacienda, Staub initially refused; he had no previous experience with Mediterranean architecture. But Mrs. Mitchell had her heart set on that style and even had sketched a tentative design on the bottom of a hatbox.

Shortly after he turned down the job, Staub traveled to Spain and Italy, where he studied local architecture. When he returned, he informed Mrs. Mitchell that he had changed his mind, and they went to work on the house. The owner contributed her ideas, and she traveled to Mexico, Spain, Portugal and Italy to shop for tiles, doors and mantels. She even brought back photographs of architectural features she admired.

The outstanding feature of the Mitchell house is the way it adapts to its hilly site. Hills are rare in Houston, and Staub immediately recognized the dramatic advantage of having the house step down, level by level, from the top of the knoll. The highest point on the ground level is the tiled entryway, with its staircase to the second floor. The baronial dining room, breakfast room and kitchen are on one side of the hall. At the end of the hall are steps down into the living room, glazed loggia and library. Another set of steps descends into the guest bedroom and bath. The multi-level floor plan creates an interesting roofline where the red tile roofs appear to overlap each other. Although it looks much larger, the house has only 13 rooms, arranged to form three sides of a garden courtyard planted with banana and mimosa trees, sago palms and azaleas. Colorful portulaca and cacti bloom in Italian and Mexican pots.

A Mexican-tiled swimming pool, patterned after pools the owner saw in Cuernavaca, reflects a fresco of the Madonna painted by French artist St. Hubert.

The house not only surrounds a garden; it is encircled by gardens as well. There is a patio garden downstairs with a Spanish wishing well more than 600 years old, an English garden behind the house and vegetable, rose and herb gardens behind that.

"It's like living in the country even though we're in the middle of the city," Mitchell explains. "We have a cage full of ring-necked doves that coo, and we've got a large population of the endangered Houston toad. They especially like our lily pond and sing loudly in unison every night."

As might be expected from an eclectic architect, the house is not purely Spanish. The grilled window near the entryway was inspired by a picture Mrs. Mitchell took of a house in Taxco, Mexico. And Staub got his idea for the unusual cornice treatment, which looks like parallel waves edging the roof, from a house he saw in Ravello, Italy. The massive front doors are 16th-century Florentine, and the ornate fireplace mantel is from Venice.

Some of the most interesting features, however, were borrowed from Spain. Particularly striking are the hand-painted tiles, reproductions of Goya's paintings, which decorate the breakfast room and form the risers and returns of the stairs in the entryway.

Mrs. Mitchell furnished the house with antiques from Europe and paintings by noted Spanish, French and Mexican artists. She leaves the tile and pegged-pine floors bare during the summer and covers them with Oriental rugs in the winter. Dark wood and crystal are accented by tapestries and brocades. The overall impression is one of elegance, the reflection of a personality as unique as the only Spanish-style house John Staub ever designed.

LEFT: A larger-than-life portrait of Dolores Mitchell hangs in the living room. It was painted on cement by French artist St. Hubert in 1941.
ABOVE: The fireplace mantel is a neoclassical marble piece from Florence, Italy; the mirrors on either side of the mantel are antiques from Mexico. A 19th-century Russian icon dominates the foreground.

ABOVE: The dining room table, from a monastery in Barcelona, Spain, is set with Capodimonte china, a pattern commissioned by Napoleon.
RIGHT: In the entrance hall, the hand-painted tiles are patterned after Goya paintings. The chest is 18th-century Spanish.

SOUTHERN PLANTATION LIVING IN TEXAS RANCH COUNTRY

After driving across miles of far West Texas' dusty desert and seeing nothing but craggy rocks, prickly pear cactus and an occasional buzzard scanning for its supper, you're almost certain your eyes must be playing a not-so-funny trick on you. The Colonial mansion rising out of the shimmering heat must be a mirage: This is Sonora, and 18th-century mansions are something of a rarity out here.

Inspired by Westover, a James River plantation house built about 1730 by William Byrd II, the Texas version is imbued with a special charm both in its graceful proportions and in its owners' unfaltering appreciation for America's heritage.

Considered by many to be America's quintessential example of Georgian architecture, Westover may seem an unlikely house to recreate in out of the way ranch country. Built on the banks where our nation was conceived and nurtured, the Virginia estate was a by-product of the fledgling frontier. Its Texas cousin, therefore, is ideally suited as a perfect complement to the country's last frontier, where the same sense of timelessness pervades and where generations of ranching families are rooted to the land and past.

The home's owner yearned to live in an 18th-century house filled with Colonial American antiques. But the realization of that dream seemed highly improbable when she married a rancher. Fortunately, he too was instilled with enthusiastic admiration for Colonial architecture and furnishings.

To design the house, the James T. Hunts relied on the professional aid of an old friend, Patrick S. Chumney of Chumney, Jones & Kell, Inc. of San Antonio. It was a project that required two years of researching Colonial restorations and extensive travel throughout New England and the South.

"I resisted doing the project at first," says Chumney. "The house was to be built in a really ludicrous setting. But they were committed to living in West Texas, and this is what they wanted to build—a large, friendly house for entertaining in the West Texas tradition."

The house is actually a combination of various characteristics from several historic sites. Millwork in the Parson Ashley House in Deerfield, Massachusetts, inspired detailing for the living room; the dining room draws its authenticity from Williamsburg. Finally, during a visit to Tidewater Virginia, the three friends toured Westover, and Chumney's clients immediately recognized the character and feeling they wanted.

Chumney's precise treatment of the exterior—steeply sloping roof, tall twin chimneys, swan's neck pediment and the three windows on either side of the front door—evoke the stately tone and classic architectural elements of the original Georgian edifice. "The house is very faithful and true to proper details," says the architect. "There's not much in the house that does not have a precedent in early American residential design."

Mrs. Hunt designed the interior and fashioned her favorite collections into a strongly personal statement. While respecting the essence of Colonial Virginia's artistic ideals, she has adapted a contemporary feeling for design with a keen sense of history, lending historical resonance to the dignified yet informal ambiance.

The Hunts' collection of colorful Oriental rugs was chosen to harmonize with the period furnishings, and the walls' gently washed shades of oyster blue and salmon were selected to match the variegated tones of the carpets. Each room has an inviting mood evoked by American wing chairs lavishly draped in silk or highlighted by striking acquisitions of Royal Crown Derby and Imari porcelains. Each personal touch of color, style and fabric reinforces the home's feeling of hospitality.

"Homes in West Texas," explains Mrs. Hunt, "are the places where we entertain. They are used for everything—our hotels, our restaurants, our tea rooms, our country clubs. They are where our children are born and where they marry."

ABOVE: Old New England is captured in an 18th-century highboy from Massachusetts. A Spode tea set, c. 1805, graces the coffee table.
RIGHT: A welcoming mood in the living room is evoked by warm pastels inspired by the time-mellowed tones of a treasured Oriental rug. Molded china niches and authentically detailed cornice molding add architectural interest.

ABOVE: Accented by a Waterford crystal chandelier, the 1790 New York mahogany dining table shines with the owners' collection of 18th-century Royal Crown Derby, reproduction Williamsburg crystal and an early American silver tea set. RIGHT: The direct view from the living room into the dining room is proof of the architectural symmetry of the house. OPPOSITE: A regal yet festive tone is set in the dining room, where a guest might believe he has been transported back to Colonial Williamsburg.

OPPOSITE: In a pleasing sense of comfort and hospitality, the kitchen admits intimate informality with its weathered cabinets, poplar beams and rustic brickwork.
ABOVE: Evoking the warm coziness of an English country inn, the pine room offers a pleasant and relaxed retreat. Furnishings include a 17th-century English drop leaf mahogany table with tall-back armchairs and wing chairs covered in a tapestry design fabric.

ABOVE: Gracefully feminine, the daughter's boudoir has a charming homespun feeling. The New England field bed, with a crocheted canopy from Massachusetts, complements a writing desk from Connecticut. and a Willard clock. A pink and white lusterware tea service adorns an early American tea table.
RIGHT: Queen Anne half-tester beds in the guest room are draped in a fresh floral fabric and accented by a Serapi rug.

FLIGHTS OF FANCY: AN UNRESTRAINED INSPIRATION

The blatant pairing of resolute opposites often creates a wonderful hybrid in which the whole is far greater than the simple sum of its parts. In fact, the newly fused entity often winds up underlining the fine contrasting qualities of its components rather than cancelling out their differences.

An elegant Colonial home in Houston offers just such a delicious counterpoint to its fashionable River Oaks neighborhood. In harmonious step with the character of surrounding architecture, a gracious Georgian facade greets passersby with fluted columns and Classical surface detail. One step through the massive front door, however, and the visitor leaves behind the ordered realm of restraint and tradition and enters instead a dazzling Oz-like wonderland of brilliant colors, upbeat furnishings and attention-getting accessories. In every aspect of design, the unexpected becomes the rule rather than the exception, and even the most insignificant corners reflect the *joie de vivre* of a magnificently audacious hand.

Few houses present a more accurate portrait of their owners than does this one belonging to Mary Ralph Lowe Yost, whose energy and imagination inspired the house's design. The portrait, however, also includes renowned Houston designer Herbert Wells, whose gift for blending color and furnishings is something of a legend in Texas. That the house was designed for a client with an innate love of color and decoration is apparent in every room. "She wanted to get away from the restriction of the traditional architecture," explains Wells.

To bring the house well into the 20th century, Wells bleached ponderous hardwood floors to a bright summery tint; to create a staccato flow between rooms, he unflinchingly drenched each in bold, intrepid colors—Viennese robin's egg blue in the dining room, cotton candy pink and cool celadon in the living room, Chinese red in the sitting room, soothing silvery grey in the sunroom. Within each of these discrete environments, the altogether unique disposition kicked off by color is complemented variously by priceless modern and Italian Renaissance art, innumerable collections—horn, crystal, porcelains and boudoir pillows—comfortable, over-scaled custom furnishings like the luxurious movable daybeds in the living room and intricately crafted antiques like the exquisite Dutch marquetry chairs in the dining room. "Mary Ralph would never buy just a straight Chippendale chair," says Wells. "It would be too dull."

In fact, everything antique, be it furniture or just a conventional structural treatment, is given a showstopping facelift. The rich patina of antique woods is rendered more dazzling by a bright contemporary fabric; molding is distinguished by a printed chintz border fabric; supposedly formal rooms are robbed of their stodginess by surprising colors and riveting artwork.

Throughout the house, there is a decidedly feminine bias. At once soft and romantic, fiery and passionate, balmy and exotic, the entire setting exudes the dreamy, enlivening spirit of the gentler sex. And yet there is also boldness at its most successful: A sunroom is adventurously latticed and canopied in shimmering silk like an Arabian palace; a separate pool house is graced by meticulously tooled wooden columns and fantastic contemporary furnishings; an otherwise overwhelming entry diverges from more traditional norms, thanks to the vivacity of a brilliant Calder mobile and the humor of a life-sized doll that perches realistically on the steps; antique wooden swans and the surreal art of Magritte create a flight of fancy in the living room.

And yet the magical poetry of the house in no way precludes streamlined common sense. There is tremendous reason amidst all the romance, and what superficially might appear flighty actually functions in a rational, orderly manner. A natural flow integrates the rooms into one kaleidoscopic space for grand-scale entertaining, while natural boundaries set up by the compartmentalized layout create a series of interesting milieux for intimate gatherings. "It's a house," says Wells, "that everybody looks wonderful in."

ABOVE: An utterly romantic, feminine retreat, the living room is an opalescent profusion of pale pinks and soothing celadons. Plush custom chaises covered in printed silk moiré can be moved about to accommodate a variety of entertaining situations. A surreal Magritte is only a preview of the dreamy fairy-tale atmosphere of the entire house. LEFT: Beautiful hand-painted antique tiles distinguish a glowing hearth. Displayed above the mantel is a dazzling Max Ernst painting. OPPOSITE: The inviting colors of an antique cotton dhurrie provide the threshold of the dining room's daring aquamarine and the living room's watercolor pinks and greens. A brilliant Calder mobile and bleached hardwood floors bring a fresh sense of modernity to the formal entry.

OPPOSITE: *Combining the best of contemporary and conventional design genius, the dining room is simultaneously exhilarating and refined. Wrapped in a hand-printed strié canvas, the room is dominated by a magnificent antique mirror. The table is composed of a mid-18th-century French steel base and a heavy marble top. Stunning 18th-century Dutch chairs are enhanced by elaborate marquetry.*
ABOVE: *A sideboard assembled to blend harmoniously with the dining room table displays an assortment of beautiful candelabra and collected Staffordshire treasures.*

ABOVE: An arresting departure from the lighthearted spirit of the rest of the house, the library is lacquered a deep Chinese red to "punch up the room," explains designer Herbert Wells. Designed as a comfortable retreat where the owner could relax and visit with her children, the room is made cozy by a Tabriz rug and assorted French chintzes in heartwarming prints. The tiny antique French child's chair is one of a special collection that figures strategically throughout the house. A battalion of Indian dolls, an antique decoy and a wooden crucifix congregate on the mantel.

OPPOSITE: Open and airy, the pool house loggia is given architectural flourish via carved freestanding columns. Accented by plump pastel pillows, casual straw and canvas furnishings are the perfect complements to surrealistic John Dickinson table designs; travertine floors bring a natural cohesion to the beachy color scheme. The striking tabletop sculpture in the foreground is by Oldenberg.

POMPEIIAN VILLA

In 1895, railroad magnate Arthur E. Stilwell founded Port Arthur as the southern terminus of his Kansas City, Pittsburgh and Gulf Railroad. Five years later, he convinced three other northern tycoons—Isaac L. Ellwood, the principal developer of barbed wire; John W. "Bet-a-Million" Gates, president of the American Steel and Wire Company; and James Hopkins, president of the Diamond Match Company—to locate their winter homes in his new town. All three men bought adjoining properties, and two of them set about building elaborate copies of homes from earlier periods. Gates chose a 20-room, Virginia-style Colonial mansion, and Ellwood opted for a 10-room Pompeiian villa. They retained Chicago architects George C. Nimmons and William K. Fellows to design and furnish their homes and to landscape their adjoining lots. Shortly after it was completed, Ellwood sold his house to James Hopkins, the St. Louis tycoon, who had never built on his original land.

Unfortunately, Hopkins made the grave error of neglecting to consult his wife, who after one brief visit returned to St. Louis, never to set foot in Port Arthur again.

Hopkins leased the house to various officials of the Guffey Petroleum Company until 1903, when banker and land developer George M. Craig asked to buy it. In trade for the house, Craig offered Hopkins his 10 percent of the stock in the newly formed Texas Company, which was capitalized for a total of $100,000. Today that corporation is known as Texaco, and Craig's $10,000 investment would be worth more than $2.2 billion.

Craig lived in the house until his death in 1950, furnishing it simply and retaining some of the original features such as the ornate brass hardware on the doors. Captain Arne Pedersen and his wife bought the villa shortly after Craig's death, but following the Pedersens' deaths in 1969 the house stood vacant. Four years later, Mrs. Pedersen's niece put the villa on the market for $60,000, then lowered the price to $50,000, then to $40,000, and finally to $30,000. Since the Gates mansion had been torn down in 1960, the villa was the last house standing from the opulent early days of Port Arthur, but it was in danger of being demolished for want of a buyer.

Sydalise Fredeman, president of the Port Arthur Historical Society, wanted to save the Pompeiian villa. First she convinced the seller to reduce the asking price to $25,000; then she raised the money. Thus the Port Arthur Historical Society was able to buy Isaac Ellwood's Pompeiian villa and begin the restoration.

The villa is a three-sided, one-story house built around a peristyle, or column-rimmed courtyard, open on one end. The exterior is almost identical to those of several villas in Pompeii, from the white Doric columns that support the portico to the latticework that rims the roof and the small windows that top the building's larger windows. The deep pink color of the exterior walls is similar to the warm tones used in Pompeii. The peristyle focuses on the Romanesque fountain. The lower two-thirds of the courtyard wall is rimmed in dark red and white molding, which was intended to border a fresco. Each of the 10 major rooms has its own door onto the peristyle, which also acts as a hall in warm weather.

The house has its original floors, which are black and white ceramic tile in the spacious entryway and longleaf pine throughout most of the house. Interior designer Charles Martin brightened the walls in the dining room, living room and French salon with gold leaf molding he unearthed in a Galveston attic. The designer painted the walls in colors he found in Pompeii: ivory for the bedrooms, grey for the French salon, peach and apricot for the entryway, ivory and cerulean blue for the living room and ivory and light almond green for the dining room.

The National Park Service placed the home on the National Register of Historic Places. The Pompeiian villa also has a state historical marker and a coveted Texas Historical Building Medallion.

Port Arthur's Pompeiian villa was built in 1900 as a winter home for the "King of Barbed Wire," Isaac Ellwood of DeKalb, Illinois. Down to the three-sided courtyard and decorative trim, the villa is a copy of a Pompeiian home of 79 A.D.
RIGHT: Roman life centered around the peristyle, a three-sided courtyard which also served as a hall, giving access to each room.

LEFT: The living room's crystal chandelier was donated by Governor Allan Shivers. The sofa is American Empire, c. 1830; the chair is one of a pair crafted by Port Arthur cabinetmaker Tim Phillips.
BELOW: A portrait of John W. "Bet-a-Million" Gates and his constant companion, a Boston bull terrier named "Blondie," hangs in the dining room. The painting is the work of late New York artist Harry Waltman, who did the portraits of several presidents. The rug is a rare French Savonnerie.

THE HIGH LIFE: VIEW FROM THE TOP

In the face of prohibitive energy costs, urban sprawl and a merciless daily pace, one essential that Texans have refused to relinquish is space: wide, open and in large parcels they can call their own. Texas is still a frontier, and land is still very much the backbone of its proud pioneer ideal. But even if Texas' land never runs out, the time in an eight-hour day does. Fewer and fewer professionals are content to append an extra two hours in commuting time to their working day. And for many homeowners, the relentless sameness of the suburbs has a wearying effect.

Gary Bebout, however, has a yard that yawns across an entire city block of one of Houston's most fashionable urban districts. "I have a pool, a jogging trail, a spring garden of azaleas and a winter one filled with zinnias and marigolds," Bebout rhapsodizes. "The only difference is that I share it with 100 people."

Bebout lives in a small, self-contained neighborhood that towers high above verdant Hermann Park. One of Houston's first high-rise condominium conversions, 1400 Hermann was constructed in the late 1950s.

Unlike many Texas homeowners, Bebout relishes the public face of high-rise living. For him, there is no confinement but all the privacy he cares to create. "I have 11 rooms of my own to wander through and 17 floors to roam if I tire of that," he says.

Bebout, publisher of *Southwest Art* magazine, is a character of many moods, and his cloud-surrounded high rise effectively paraphrases a richly diversified lifestyle brimming with exciting people, exquisite art and eclectic collections.

An intriguing synthesis of three separate apartments, his skytop home rambles aesthetically around an upper corner of the building; with every opened door, a new world unfolds, each with a distinctly different flavor and each suitable to an intended function. At every turn, first-time guests, feeling certain the next door can only lead to a linen closet, are delighted to find it spills onto yet another attractive hideaway. Old friends, however, have favorite rooms they seek out on every visit. Designed by Richard Miller of Suniland, the unusual fusion of the three layouts establishes a flow that accommodates parties of more than 100. Yet the mere closing of doors creates an intimacy rarely matched in larger houses.

Curiously, the entrance leads directly onto a breakfast room where quiet beige and apricot tones are welcoming and subdued. As a foyer, its atmosphere is regal; and when a small marble table is set, the passageway nature of the entry provides a refreshing, open area for morning meals.

A step to the left unfurls a romantic formal dining room. Against the neon night, lavish red silk chairs are reflected in bronze-mirrored walls to create an opulent backdrop for gourmet dining. Conversely, a step to the right gives access to the comfortable, subtly shaded master bedroom and sitting room. Restfully decorated, they form a stunning repository for Bebout's collection of Lalique and Baccarat crystal and Chinese porcelains, which also strategically adorn tabletops, pedestals and breakfronts throughout the apartment. An extensive array of 17th- and 18th-century European and contemporary American paintings weaves muted colors into the thoughtful design.

Removed from that central wing, past a chrome- and mirror-studded kitchen, another bedroom and the chinchilla-colored library, is a setting for serious entertainment, an ambiance where Bebout's sole intention is that his guests kick their shoes off and sing, dance and carouse far into the night. Dominated by a sparkling 15-foot bar and a baby grand piano, the room's beige tones are jazzed up at regular intervals with arresting splashes of fire engine red.

A culmination of years of collecting and selecting fine art, furniture and accessories, the lofty residence is also the result of years of different habitats. "I've moved 15 times in the past 18 years," says Bebout. "After trying everything from low-rise townhouses to duplexes and apartments to houses to high rises," he laughs, "I'd never live on the ground again."

thwest Art

LEFT: In the master sitting room, a custom sofa sits in front of a mirrored coffee table showcasing part of Bebout's collection of Lalique crystal. Subtle tones prevail in the master suite, which offers a year-round view of Hermann Park and the downtown skyline.
ABOVE: In the entry, a Chinese chest is flanked by two Empire-style chairs of deep green leather.

ABOVE: With its deep Chinese-red color scheme, the dining room is a jewel box that opens onto a glittering skyline.
OPPOSITE: The formal table is set with Lalique and antique rose-point crystal, Chinese export dinnerware and opulent silver. An assemblage of silver objets de vertu *provides an elegant counterpoint to the dazzling view.*

Kimball

OPPOSITE: An intriguing synthesis of three separate apartments, this high-rise home rambles comfortably to establish a flow that accommodates parties of more than 100. The entertainment room, dominated by a baby grand piano, is spiced with pillows in bright red silk.
ABOVE: Displaying such treasures as early 18th-century Chinese hat stands, a Satsuma vase and celadon plates, a Regency console creates a stunning vignette. The mirror is Venetian glass.

SOPHISTICATED DESIGNS FOR PRIMITIVE ARTS

In the home, beauty that sneaks up from behind rather than overwhelming the eye always seems to result from an elusive knack for achieving subtlety. Rare are the souls who, without a formal recipe, can mix colors and scales and moods, voids and solids and space to create a perfect ensemble of the avant-garde as well as tasteful understatement.

The casual attitude governing designer David Corley's vast collection of primitive arts and crafts spills over into his general design philosophy and into his hilltop Fort Worth house proper. "If you leave something in one place long enough," muses the partner in the Fort Worth firm Minton-Corley, "you begin to take it for granted and stop seeing it, no matter how unusual it is. That's why we move things around so much. It's fun to see a piece in a different light—and to see the different light it sheds on its new surroundings."

While the collection provides a decorative touchstone for the house, it possesses not a shred of sterility nor the least hint of curatorial intimidation. Similar pieces are not grouped behind glass; neither are they mounted slavishly in chronological order. Instead, Corley and his wife scoot individual treasures around to suit their whims. For that reason, the visitor to the house feels no hands-off museum constriction upon entering; instead of being taken aback by the assertiveness of such a magisterial exhibition, he perceives the collection piecemeal—comfortably, almost imperceptibly, noticing only the perfect punctuation here and there of an interesting color, texture or shape.

"I like the straightforward honesty and simplicity of folk art from all cultures," says Corley of his open-ended battery of pre-Columbian ceramics, Eskimo carvings, American Indian weavings and basketry, Himalayan artifacts, Greek pottery and American folk art. Not unexpectedly, these same characteristics also epitomize his house. While the quality of both the collection and its setting is a foregone conclusion, there is nary a trace of snobbery about it. Comfortable, functional materials and groupings beckon rather than humble, and while there is no lack of captivating drama, it is not altogether unapparent that the house was drafted with a large family in mind. Utterly elegant and sophisticated in its use of colors and design, the entire house bespeaks an uncomplicated, comfortable lifestyle full of easygoing entertaining and the relaxed appreciation of a lifelong collection of antiques.

When purchased seven years ago the house was a 20-year-old "typically Texas non-architectural structure," Corley explains. "It had no style, really." To lighten and open the design so as to capitalize on a setting overlooking the Trinity River, Corley stretched French doors across the front and back, laid bleached oak floors and washed all the rooms with an uplifting coat of paint.

"I don't like a house that looks decorated," he explains. "Therefore I never had any real preconceived notion of what the house would become. It just evolved around the things we like. And we like and use everything we have."

And so it appears, with absolutely nothing contrived about it. The key throughout is balance, achieved naturally and without artifice. The lustrous patina and curvilinear contours of exquisite antiques successfully disarm the harshness that might have resulted from too much cold geometry.

Clean lines and contemporary shapes, on the other hand, avoid the cloying nostalgia that is so often part and parcel of period interiors. High-quality wicker suits the daytime informality of the sunroom, while custom contemporary furniture against dark, lacquered walls creates a smashing evening aura in the living room. In the bedroom, light, refreshing colors and clean lines, neither distinctly masculine nor emphatically feminine, are soothing to the tired eye, while sumptuous marble, modern leather seating and bookshelves brimming with volumes and valuables give rise to a sybaritic sanctuary in the master bath.

ABOVE: The sunroom is an unpretentious blend of wicker upholstered in canvas sailcloth and peppered with batik pillows, folk art and contemporary paintings. A large Zia pot, part of an American Indian collection, sits beside the sofa; the painting above the fireplace is by Julio Larraz.
OPPOSITE: A cotton dhurrie and a whimsical painting by David Ligare echo the sunlit tones beaming in from outside. Actually a French dough bin, the coffee table is but one of the collectibles that vie for attention: The 19th-century Boston fishmonger's sign sits atop a 17th-century Northern Italian chest, while a Connecticut horse weathervane cuts a charming silhouette against the window.

ABOVE: In the dining room, a Normandy buffet displays antique pewter and ironstone from the British Isles. Rough-hewn tree-branch chairs with rush seats are a pleasant counterpoint to walls upholstered in silk batiks.
RIGHT: Extra-wide, comfortably skirted chairs and sofa by Minton-Corley, Audubon prints and a Jim Blake oil are dazzling against the flattering tobacco-lacquered walls in the living room. A pre-Columbian parrot bowl sits atop the coffee table, and a Himalayan temple drum serves as a creative end table.

ABOVE: *With contemporary lines softened considerably by shirring and skirting, Minton-Corley designs in the master bedroom are neither decidedly feminine nor emphatically masculine. Soft colors combine to soothe the eye while art, largely by contemporary Italian artists, offers engaging surface detail.*
OPPOSITE: *A harem window next to the door cleverly caches the television set; Eskimo sculptures and a Julio Larraz painting are among the collectibles that populate the relaxing haven.*

PROVOCATIVE DRAMA: GEOMETRY AND ROMANCE

After a lifetime of traditional houses replete with elaborate moldings, beautifully mullioned windows, carved cornices and period appointments, the prospect of life in a pared-down contemporary habitat can often be unsettling. For one Houston homeowner, however, the dramatic departure of soaring spaces, assertive geometry and a flood of daylight seemed a desirable change of atmosphere—providing certain criteria were met.

Security was a major concern to the owner. And as long as softening elements were incorporated to the advantage of a lifelong collection of elegant antiques and stunning artwork, the notion of a fortified contemporary was acceptable.

To obtain a livable shelter that satisfied those specific aesthetic and functional requirements, the owner approached two of the state's design luminaries: Midland architect Frank Welch and Houston designer Herbert Wells, who have waved wizards' wands over some of Texas' most fashionable homes.

In direct response to the need for extra security, the house is a private haven that presents to the street a rampart-like natural stucco wall. But to avoid what Welch terms "a paranoid appearance" as well as to alleviate the relentless planar surface of the outer wall, decorative grillwork and treillage on an upstairs balcony, a keeping room and around the pool add the interesting surface detail often lacking in ultra-modern projects.

The owner expressly desired a large, important social space with a good deal of natural light. Although an architectural wonder of massive scope, the joint living room/dining room, with lofty 20-foot ceilings and gaping windows atop sliding glass doors, presented Wells a challenge in scale that might, in fact, have totally stymied a designer of lesser resourcefulness. Relating magnificent painted antique furniture—principally of Italian and French origin—to such a cavernous space could have spelled disaster for a strong, very pivotal collection. But details like an extra-large custom sofa, an enormous hand-crafted iron chandelier and great tin downspouts joined and hung against the towering dining room wall above an Italian bibliothèque help fill the potentially amorphous space.

In addition, Wells relied on the velveteen softness of a greige and peach color wheel to accentuate the beautiful painted veneers and to absorb the otherwise blinding light that streams in from a multitude of angles. "If the walls had been whitewashed," he explains, "the house would have been nothing more than a museum."

Balancing the large, open living area, a cozy keeping room adjacent to the spacious working kitchen offers an alternative to the decidedly contemporary feel of the more public rooms. In a hall connecting the keeping room and the bedroom area, antique French doors add age and character to streamlined contemporary contours. Private and small, the bedrooms are elegantly subtle and give convenient access to a beautiful Greek-style pool that also becomes a dazzling mural across the width of the living room.

Throughout, flooring of Mexican travertine pavers provides a cool common denominator for the conglomeration of English, French and Italian antiques, large-scale contemporary artwork and assorted collections ranging from Mexican santos to antique porcelains to rock crystal to great fossilized fungi.

The pairing of clean, contemporary geometry with particularly sumptuous, romantic furnishings and accessories is roundly successful in this comfortable abode; neither the excitement of the architecture nor the period value of the appointments is diminished, and the resulting package is one that allures without intimidation or saccharine nostalgia.

"The owner," says Frank Welch, "is a delightful woman who profits to the maximum from every aspect of life. She loves to cook and entertain, loves music and art and people." With its provocative architectural drama, ethereal gossamer palette and eclectic furnishings, the exquisite house is a fitting backdrop for a gracious Texas hostess.

PRECEDING PAGES: *With its glowing palette, a Helen Frankenthaler oil is a pivotal cornerstone in the color scheme of the expansive living room. Large custom sofas and a Louis XVI canapé delineate a comfortable seating area around the antique French marble mantel. To fill the yawning, sunlit space in the two-story room, a massive fronded chandelier was fashioned from bits and pieces of antique Italian metalwork.*
ABOVE: *In an unexpectedly elegant combination, Hepplewhite chairs surround a table of faux marble on a Directoire steel base. Sprays of calla lilies are displayed in antique French tin cemetery vases.*
OPPOSITE: *A painted Italian bibliothèque houses a collection of assorted antique porcelains. Above it, twin tin downspouts rescued from the wrecking ball create a striking cornice that equalizes the scale of furnishings and towering space.*

ABOVE: Although greenhouse skylights with convenient motorized shades usher in an abundance of overhead light, intricate whitewashed latticework ensures both privacy and security in the sunroom. With its cool travertine floors and hand-printed canvas-upholstered furnishings, the corner offers a casual departure from the sleekly refined living and dining rooms.
OPPOSITE: Dramatic by day, the house assumes fantastic glamour by night, pierced as it is by oversized windows; lit from within, it appears a giant shimmering jack-o-lantern against the secluded flagstone-paved pool area. Fountains play to create stunning water sculpture when the pool is not in use for exercise.

High Profile

Fete Set

More Fete Set on page 14

By Jann Kelso

WHERE: Home of Sigmund Mandell.
WHEN: Dec. 9.
WHAT: *Texas Homes* magazine hosted a cocktail party and preview of its new book, *The Grand Homes of Texas.*
WHO:
Above: Sigmund Mandell and Mary and David Corley (from left).
Right: Blaine Hickey, *Texas Homes* publisher Ann Richardson and Ogden Robertson (from left).